NEW MONOLOGUES

FOR

WOMEN

BY

WOMEN

NEW MONOLOGUES

FOR

WOMEN

BY

WOMEN

EDITED BY TORI HARING-SMITH & LIZ ENGELMAN

HEINEMANN
Portsmouth, NH

Heinemann
A division of Reed Elsevier Inc.
361 Hanover Street
Portsmouth, NH 03801–3912
www.heinemanndrama.com

Offices and agents throughout the world

Performance rights material can be found on page 156.

Library of Congress Cataloging-in-Publication Data
New monologues for women by women / edited by Tori Haring-Smith and Liz Engelman.
p. cm.
Includes index.
ISBN 0-325-00626-1 (alk. paper)
1. Monologues. 2. Acting—Auditions. 3. American drama—20th century. 4. Women—Drama. I. Haring-Smith, Tori. II. Engelman, Liz.
PN2080.N49 2004
808.82'45'080082—dc22   2004001419

Editor: Lisa A. Barnett
Production coordinator: Elizabeth Valway
Production service: Lisa S. Garboski, bookworks
Typesetter: Tom Allen/Pear Graphic Design
Cover design: Jenny Jensen Greenleaf
Manufacturing: Steve Bernier

Printed in the United States of America on acid-free paper
08 07 06 05 04   VP   1 2 3 4 5

Contents

Subject Index

Sex and Desire

Violence and Revenge

Most of the monologues in this collection can be performed by actors of any age, but those listed below are particularly well suited for younger or more senior women by virtue of their subject matter, situation, or language.

Monologues Particularly Suited for Actors under 20

Axler, By Definition
Bagatourian, The Strawberry Scene
Berman, Winter with Tambourine Boy
Congdon, So Far
DiNovelli, The Four Effs
Harrington, Excerpt from *Do You Have Time to Die?*
Hunter, Excerpt from *Distance Over Time Equals*
McLaughlin, Excerpt from *Iphigenia and Other Daughters*
Reingold, Circus Madness
Shamieh, The Black Eyed
Swanson, God Is Kind to Some Women

Monologues Particularly Suited for Actors Older than 60

Allard, Arm Bone
Bridgforth, Excerpt from *con flama*
Derrickson, Addicts
Dial, Circles
Grantham, Take Back the Classroom
Jaspers, Anymore
Porter, Netty's Dance
Ralli, Gone Stone Cold
Wylie, Breathing Space

Why Monologues?

Why monologues, you ask? Why *another* collection of monologues, and why yet another collection by *women*?

A monologue is conversation. A monologue is not a soliloquy, nor is it a speech. No internal struggles, no pontification. Rather, a monologue is action. It can effect change. It can take you on a journey. It can tell a good story—a story that needs telling now. It can persuade, convince, entice, confess. It can seduce. It can ask a question, it can make a demand.

We have assembled fifty-nine monologues by the most exciting voices that exist today, voices from all over the globe, though not always all over our stages. Once again, it is time for these voices—old and new—to be heard by others. We are all familiar with production statistics that place women's work on the lower end of the production spectrum. It is an old tune that sings the blues of women underrepresented on the mainstages across the country. This melancholy tune does not reflect, however, the deep range of women's voices ready to be recognized. In this volume, we have captured only a small sample of the vibrancy resonating in the words of women writing today, from both emerging writers yet to be known and those that already are familiar to theatre goers.

Whatever your age, ethnicity, background, or taste, we hope that when you pick up this book, somewhere in the volume of work represented here there is a monologue that speaks to—and for—you and that you find in the specifics penned on the page connections to share with others from the stage. Whether they are relating to food (you know us women), class, men (they'll never go away), family (they don't go away either), or a favorite pet, the characters within these pages use humor, metaphor, and their own colorful idiosyncrasies to reveal the familiar in the unfamiliar—and vice versa. It is in these unusual looks at their lives that we are able to catch a good glimpse of our own life's great truths.

As you read, remember: a monologue is only one side of the conversation. Someone else is listening. Who is that someone? A lover? A soon-to-be ex? Your mother? Your boss? Why are you talking to them? Are you breaking up? Coming together? Asking forgiveness? Quitting your job? As importantly, why are you telling them now?

Well, why not? Jump in, take a journey, make a change, make sure you get what you want. And maybe laugh, or cry, or learn a little along the way, all in a paragraph or a page or two. Pretty incredible, isn't it? Go ahead. Give voice to these women's words from around the world. Thank them for their scored notes, and they'll thank you for playing them with your live instrument.

—Liz Engelman, Tori Haring-Smith

Tips on Auditioning with a Monologue

Choosing a Monologue

In order to perform a monologue well, you should have some personal connection to it. You need to understand the character's emotion and be passionate about her concerns. After all, you are going to have to explore this character in depth and then generate enough energy to make her live for your audience. In some cases, actors are drawn to monologue characters because they have undergone similar experiences. If the character is talking about death and you have recently lost a loved one, you may be able to share something of yourself—your grief—through bringing the character to life. Remember, acting is about sharing yourself. That's one reason why actors must learn to be vulnerable and to relax. When you audition, your audience wants to know who you are, as well as who you can be. Your choice of a monologue often reveals you, so choose carefully.

It is common advice that monologues should talk about the present, not just recount memories from the past. We think this advice, although well intentioned, is artificially limiting. There is nothing wrong with a monologue that tells a story from the past as long as you, the actor, make it present and active. As long as the story is a vital part of the character you develop, it will stir emotions, shape interactions, and reveal layers within the character. Remember that all monologues have at least one silent stage partner, someone who is listening and responding to the character, perhaps driving the character to keep speaking. Sometimes the silent partner is another character, sometimes another facet of the speaker, and sometimes the theatre audience. As long as a monologue connects with your passions, you will be able to make it live for your silent stage partner and for your audience.

Even though a monologue springs from the interaction of two characters, it must not be too dependent on the context of the play if it is going to stand on its own in an audition. That is, the monologue needs to make sense and be important in its own right—not because of its function within the play as a whole. Many of the most exciting monologues in full-length plays simply cannot stand on their own, because in isolation they do not reveal the character fully enough. Most successful audition monologues do not refer to too many people other than the speaker. It's difficult to keep track of a woman's lover, husband, daughter, and business associate all in one two-minute monologue! The primary purpose of a monologue is to showcase you, not the play or the playwright. If a monologue is well chosen, it should not require any introduction beyond the title of the play.

It is important that a monologue (or a pair of monologues, if you are performing two together) allows you to show a range of emotional, physical, and vocal qualities. Although you can get some range by choosing a pair of contrasting monologues, each piece you do should have variety within it. The emotional state of the character needs to be dynamic, so that you can show more than one side of your emotional, physical, and vocal life. If you are choosing a pair of monologues, you will probably want to find speeches on different subjects as well with differing tones.

When choosing a monologue, you should try to find material that will be new to your audience. When we audition large numbers of people, we hear the same monologues over and over again. Sometimes we can hardly listen to painfully familiar pieces such as the twirler from *In the Boom-Boom Room*. When you choose a classical monologue, think about how many Juliets or Kates your auditioners will have heard on the professional stage and in auditions. Try to find some new material. Women playwrights from the medieval period,

Renaissance, Restoration, and eighteenth century are just now being rediscovered and published. Look for collections of their works, and you may find wonderful new monologues. Although *New Monologues for Women by Women* will not help you find a classical monologue, it will provide you with more than fifty previously unpublished or very hard-to-find contemporary pieces.

Be sure that the monologue is suitable for you as well as for the theatre or film for which you are auditioning. This does not mean that the character needs to match you identically in race, gender, age, or geographical location. Just be sure that you understand the character and how she responds to life. If you feel that you would respond as she does, you probably have a sympathetic relationship to the character. If you are playing someone much older or younger than yourself, do not simply "play age"—play yourself. Also avoid pieces that require a strong accent, unless you are told that you need to demonstrate particular dialect abilities. Some people have an accented piece in their storehouse of "extra" monologues—those that are not their primary audition pieces but are available if auditioners want to see more.

Think about the suitability of your monologue for the medium in which you are auditioning. If you are being seen for television work, the monologue should be rated PG. If you have been called for a particular role, try to find a monologue that is generally similar to that script or role (i.e., use a comic piece if you're auditioning for a comedy) but is not from the script itself. The auditioners will have all kinds of preconceived notions about the roles they are casting. If you pull a monologue from the play they have been dreaming about for several months, you may not seem right to them if your interpretation of the character does not match their ideal for it. If the auditioners want to see you in the part, they will ask for a cold reading.

Finally, think about the length of your monologues. Do not cram so much into your two or three minutes that you feel rushed while you are performing. Respect the time limits set by the auditioners. Some of the monologues in this book are obviously too long to be done in an audition, and you will have to cut them. But having access to the entire monologue gives you a fuller sense of context as well as offering you material for longer performance in showcases and workshops.

Preparing and Rehearsing

As you rehearse your monologue, either alone or with a coach, use the techniques that have been most successful for you in preparing full-length roles. If the piece is from a longer work, read that play. But do not rely on the longer work to "explain" the character—after all, your auditioners may not know the piece. The monologue must stand on its own as a comprehensible piece, telling the auditioners all they need to know about your character. Also, don't let the full play's context limit you. Don't assume that because the character in the play is insane, your interpretation must also reveal insanity. More important than any research in the library, more important even than reading the full script, is careful examination of the specific text that you are going to present. Think about the character drawn there and ask yourself the usual character-development questions, including:

- Who is this person talking to? Does that shift at any point during the piece? What does the listener want from the speaker?
- What question or event is the speaker responding to? What happened just before she began to speak?
- What does the speaker need? Why does she keep on speaking? (Make this need as important as possible.)
- What are the conflicts within the speaker and between the speaker and her listener(s)?
- What does the speaker's language reveal about her? What

is the speaker's favorite word in this monologue?
- How is the speaker different after she has said her piece than before? What has she gained, lost, discovered?
- What line in the monologue is the most important? Where does the speech make emotional turns? Where does it reach a climax?

As you explore the character, keep reassuring yourself that you are not necessarily looking for the "right" answers to your character questions. You are looking for emotionally truthful answers that you can play. Be faithful to your own experience and your own sense of truth—not to what someone else thinks that the character "should" be like. Do not be satisfied with quick, easy answers. Keep probing.

As you work on the character, consider her vocal and physical life. Would she sit down, or is she too overwrought? Does she try to hide her strong emotions behind civilized, controlled speech, or does she speak out? Experiment with different business you might give the character as well. Is she knitting while she talks? Is she fidgeting with a button? Putting on makeup? Consider her body stance. Does she stand tall? Hunch forward? Sit primly? Be sure that you make choices that allow you to keep your head up and that do not force you to move so frenetically than the auditioners cannot "see" you for the movement. Know where your silent partner is. Do not make the auditioner a silent partner—no one wants to be forced to participate in an actor's piece. Does the silent partner move at any point? Where, when, and how?

As you rehearse, concentrate on your primary goal of making the character present and active. Command attention—think of what Linda Loman says about Willy—"Attention must be paid." If you know what the character wants, then you will have no trouble bringing that need out for the audience.

Once you begin to put your actual performance together, consider how you will start. Your introduction of yourself and your piece are part of the performance, because you are in fact "on" from the moment that you walk through the doors of the audition room or onto the stage. Practice introducing yourself pleasantly and efficiently:

> Hello. My name is _____, and today I'll be doing monologues from Darrah Cloud's *Braille Garden* and Mary Pix's *The Innocent Mistress*.

Then work on the transition into your first monologue. Take a moment to visualize your character's situation, to ground yourself in her needs, to place your silent partner, and to think about the question or event to which you are responding. Practice this kind of preparation, and you will not need more than five seconds to accomplish it.

Work through the transitions between monologues in the same way. After you have chosen an order for your pieces, consider how you will move smoothly from one to the other. Be sure that you complete the first monologue, and give it a beat to sink in, then alter your physicality in some way and quickly launch into the second piece. As you rehearse, have someone time your work. Be sure that you are well within the time limits set by the audition. When you are performing, you want to be able to think about the character, not the clock. Take your time to live the character fully but not self-indulgently. And, above all, don't be afraid of being boring. If you think you're boring, you're going to telegraph that to your auditioners, and your worst nightmare will come true.

Plan what you are going to wear to the audition. Think of something that complements your body type and doesn't distort your presentation of either of your characters. You do not want to look costumed during your audition; you want to look as much like yourself as you can. The goal of the audition is to reveal yourself and the range of your abilities. You may want to costume one character by adding or taking off a jacket or scarf, but do not plan elaborate costume changes. Most people do not change costume at all during their auditions. After all, you should be able to present the character without relying on a costume to support you. Similarly, you may need one small prop in one of your monologues—a pencil, a book. If you need more props than that, you have not chosen an appropriate audition piece. Remember that the only furniture you can count on having is a folding metal chair. Try to be as self-sufficient as possible and not to rely on costumes, props, or furniture. Your acting—not the technical aspects of your performance—must be the focus. Your auditioners should remember you, not your costume.

As you rehearse, keep exploring. Take risks—that's what rehearsals are for. If you find that you are afraid of looking foolish—playing either too big or too small—face your fears. Do the monologue as you fear it might be seen at its very worst. Facing your fears helps them dissolve away. But if you don't face them, enact them, and experience your worst nightmare in the safety of a rehearsal, your fears will limit your spontaneity and make you censor yourself. Sometimes you will discover that your worst nightmare may have been an excellent choice for the piece—you were just afraid of taking the chance. Don't be afraid to be quirky or bold.

Some people hire coaches to help them prepare monologue work. Whether you rehearse alone or with a coach, at some point you need to practice performing your work in front of different audiences. Don't always practice or perform in the same place. Move around. Get used to performing anywhere, so that the strangeness of the audition situation will not throw you. If you can perform with equal concentration and comfort in a living room, on a stage, in a classroom, and out of doors, you're probably well prepared for your audition.

Presenting Yourself and Your Work

Before your audition, try not to establish expectations. Of course, you should be aware of any rules that have been set for the audition—number of pieces you should present, time limits, requirements for the types of monologues—but don't establish expectations for the audition process itself. Don't "picture" the room, because you may then be surprised, and you'll have to deal with that surprise when you should be acting. If you think, "Oh, I'll be up on a big stage in a 2,000-seat auditorium" and you end up auditioning in a hotel conference room, you'll have trouble making immediate adjustments, and doing so will distract you from concentrating on the monologue.

Don't even make assumptions about the behavior or the number of the people who will be watching you. Sometimes you will be performing for one person, sometimes for fifty or sixty in combined auditions such as Strawhat or Midwest Theatre Auditions. Don't anticipate rapt attention from your auditors. They may look at your intently, they may eat while your perform (they often don't get lunch breaks), or they may pass papers around or talk about you. Don't be surprised, don't be thrown. Just do your work and let them do theirs. It is hard not to be offended if someone is talking while you perform, but keep your concentration on your own work. Remember, they may be saying, "She's perfect for the part, isn't she?"

Get a good night's sleep before your audition and wear comfortable clothes. If you're going on a callback, wear the same or similar clothes that you wore to the first audition. If the auditioners liked that person, they will both remember and like a similar looking one during callbacks. Wearing a T-shirt and jeans to an initial audition and then a suit to the callbacks only confuses the people who are trying to find the real you. Bring extra copies of your picture and résumé in case you need them.

Know where you are going and give yourself plenty of time to get there. You don't want to be nervous about your punctuality. You may have forms to fill out, and you will want to warm up before you audition. Find a quiet space to center yourself, warm up vocally and physically, and run over your piece to be sure that you are comfortable with it. If you can't find a private space, just close your eyes, focus, and take yourself through the piece in your head. Follow the emotional track of the character and visualize your silent partner. In other words, perform in your head. This is the same practice that professional athletes engage in when they visualize themselves making a free throw or kicking a goal before they act.

When it is time for you to audition, you will be admitted into the audition room by a monitor or the casting director. In most cases, you or the casting director will have sent your picture and résumé to the director. If not, then hand the picture and résumé to the director as you enter the room and cross to the audition area. If the director initiates a conversation, respond politely and efficiently. Think of this a cocktail conversation. Most directors, though, will not initiate conversation. They're rushed, and they just want to see who you are.

As soon as you enter the room, seize the space. Walk confidently and know that for the next three minutes, you are in charge of what happens in that space. It is all too easy to experience auditions as a kind of meat market, in which you are just a number. In fact, auditions are often like this, but you must never present yourself as "just one more actor." Take the stage. Know you're important.

If you need to move a chair or set up the space, do so quickly. Then pause to be sure that the director is ready for you to proceed. In some cases, a monitor will indicate when you should begin. Introduce yourself and your piece, making eye contact with the director or with as many of a large group of directors as possible. This is the only time during the formal part of the audition that you should make direct eye contact with the auditioners. Set up your space so that you are facing the auditioners, but put your silent partner to one side of them or just behind them. Once your introduction is over, take a few seconds (no more) to focus completely on your work and then go.

At the end of the performance, wait a beat, break character, and then say, "Thank you." If, for some reason, the director wants to see more of you, you may be asked to do a cold reading or additional monologues. Always have some additional work in reserve. It is not uncommon, especially in graduate school auditions, for directors to request specific types of monologues. "Do you have something more upbeat?" "Can you show us a more vulnerable character?" "Do you have something in verse?" You can never be prepared for all requests, but have a supply of work at your beck and call. If you are not asked to do additional work, however, don't be depressed. You may not have suited the role, or you may have been so perfect that the auditioners know immediately that they want to see you at callbacks.

When you've finished, never comment on your own work—especially to apologize. The most important thing is to be confident and to look like you're having a good time throughout the audition. Don't even comment on your own work by scowling, frowning, or shrugging as you walk away.

Once you have left the audition, try not to second-guess the director. Even if the director seemed to respond well to your work, don't begin to fantasize about what it will be like to work with that director or on that project. If you don't get the part, you'll just be doubly disappointed. Every actor needs a strong support system. You put yourself on the line daily—you are the product that you are selling—and although you may know that not everyone wants or needs your product, it is never easy to take rejection. Remember that even famous actors face rejection every day. Keeping faith in yourself and in those around you who stay by you in your times of need will see you through and keep you sane.

Auditioning is an actor's job. It can be a nightmare, but it can also be fun. You meet lots of different people, get tips on upcoming projects, and have a chance, however brief, to perform. Just keep reminding yourself that you are in control of your performance. No matter how good you are, you will be right only for some roles. Can you imagine Roseanne Arnold as a sensitive figure skater? Keep true to your own sense of self, keep polishing your acting skills, and be sure that you have other ways of measuring your self-worth aside from getting cast in any one given role.

Geoffrey

JOAN ACKERMANN

DARLENE: Am I mad? Mad? Why, do I look mad? Yeah. I'm mad. I'm mad. *Why* am I mad? Mm? Speak a little more clearly, you're swallowing your drool, e-nun-ci-ate. (*Pause*) Let me translate . . . You're asking me am I mad because you're two hours late, dinner's cold, you just parked your big-ass ugly Bronco on the garden border I spent the whole entire afternoon putting in, is that why I'm mad? (*Pause*) Garden . . . border. It is a foot high "border" for the "garden," it's decorative, tasteful, people who have class, people who care about their appearances have them, a little midget white charming picket fence. (*Pause*) No. That's correct, you are correct, we don't have a garden and this is because you and your brother who shares your genes park your trucks all the fuck anywhere you want right up the back door hence there is no grass, there is no garden, which is why I put a garden border in, CONCEPT, CONCEPT, which cost thirty-nine dollars and now exists no more under those great big overkill tires you so desperately need to ride high upon. (*Pause*) How do I know? Have you ever heard of a "window," Geoffrey, it is a gazing device through which you gain insight, observation, into the outer planet, the world that is happening out there unlike the vast nothing that is happening continuously, repeatedly, nonstop over and over and over in your mind. (*Pause*) You're right. You're right, the new garden border wasn't there this morning, you are now projecting the appearance of someone who is thinking, trying to project the information that because it wasn't there when you left is why you screeched back to the edge of our house without looking down. Without looking down. Very correct, it wasn't there this

I

morning, it got here today all afternoon when I was down on my knees, my knees, digging, sweating, scraping down through dirt with rocks, stones so big I had to dig around them and remove them, dig deep enough to put the border in but not too deep so enough of it, the same amount, was sticking up all the way along, all the way along, while the entire time Gretchen, inside the house, was hysterical because her goldfish overheated on the windowsill and we buried it and you're probably parked on that too. AND—you're not going anywhere, don't think you're going anywhere—and . . . also through the window I gained the information of the group death of forty-two baby beautiful impatiens plants, forty-two, six to a pack, color-coordinated, pink purple white, pink purple white, pink purple white, I planted next to the garden border which you also crushed and killed and maimed in your haste to get here two hours late. But that's not why I'm mad. That's not why I'm mad. I'm mad, I'm mad, Geoffrey, because it's Tuesday. That's why I'm mad. Plain and simple. Because it's Tuesday. You can take that and do with it what you please.

Cantaloupe

LIZ DUFFY ADAMS

OK, listen. I mean it, darlings, shut your adorable yaps and open your great flapping ears and list while I speak. I woke up this morning—OK, this afternoon—OK, OK, what do you want from me, *just* at that Magritte twilight moment—and there was a taste of cantaloupe in my mouth. And I thought . . . what did I think . . . I didn't think: I wondered I puzzled I big-fat PANICKED I subsided . . . Because you see, darlings, I haven't had a cantaloupe in more than donkey years—*herds* of donkey years—great thundering stampeding wild crazed drunken *burro* years—so you see. Where did that taste come from, what was it doing in my mouth, the smell of it in my by-now desperately flaring nostrils, the Proustian kick of it hammering at my cantaloupe-remembering brain? Because I once loved cantaloupe. Cantaloupe has accompanied for me some of those days you hope you remember as you die, some of those memories you summon up as the plane is going down—at least that's my plan—to keep from dying badly, gracelessly, *vulgarly,* frankly, though that's an obsolete concept, vulgarity, it's a vulgar universe and that's fine, darlings, honestly. *But.* It's a universe without cantaloupes in it. It's been a cantaloupe-absent world for as long as I can count, and I'm very, very good at counting. They're gone, those rough dusty globes filled with moist, tender, cantaloupe-colored flesh. Gone, gone, gone. Along with melon-ballers, and prosciutto, and toothpicks, and Sunday brunches and mimosas and just about everyone who still knows what cantaloupe tasted like. So. You see, my darlings. I know we're not supposed to panic, I know it's unpatriotic to panic. The small god Pan is gone too, packed his Louis Vuitton and moved to Mars or wherever and there's no point in panicking. I would have thought my adrenal glands were no longer capable of it, actually, darlings. Aren't yours? But in that dark blue twilight moment, I thought, I wondered, I puzzled, I panicked . . . because bad as a world without cantaloupe may be, *is,* darlings, what might be worse, what might just be scale-tippingly, break the drunken burro's back worse, is a world haunted by the ghosts of cantaloupes past. No, that's not what I thought, I lie. I thought, *what smells like cantaloupe? What am I breathing? Is the plane going down, is it time to remember those days and hope to be reborn on a planet without people?* But I'm still here. So I guess it was just a ghostly melon, the spirit of a vine-ripened extinct fruit, haunting me. Imagine that. Lick your lips and think of that.

Arm Bone

JANET ALLARD

A woman stands over her sleeping daughter. She has been dead two years.

You so lazy, it's late already, get out of bed. You know what today is, you wouldn't forget. You wouldn't forget my two-year anniversary! Been dead two years, time flies. Rapai! Yes, it's me. Your mum! Don't look so surprised to see me. There's something you need to do. You know your Uncle Dollar? Not really your Uncle, yeah, but you know you called him that, you know he was my only true, of course your father and I, but he and I, we were music, he was the drum, I was, you know, he was my only, I miss the sex, I know it's the last thing you want to hear, but the sex, Rapai, HOOOOOOO. I hope, in your lifetime you get to have sex like, you wouldn't think, because he's so short and ugly but WHOOOOOOOOO. How is he, Rapai? Do you see him? Does he sing still? That song. That song we loved. How does it go? About the woman who's dead but she visits her lover every night, and he always said, when I'm dead I'll—

There's something I need you to do, to give him. He wanted. Rapai— So we can still. Make music together. My arm bone. Don't look away, don't make that face. Listen. My arm bone, this one, you heard me, my arm bone. I promised it to Uncle Dollar, Rapai, that face. You heard me, listen. I promised it to him so he could make a flute. A flute. Listen. And play my body, listen. The way he used to play my body, listen. When we were together, Rapai, his lips, his fingers, his breath, listen, our voices together, listen. You stubborn. Listen. What's the big deal? All you got to do is dig. Get a

5

shovel and dig. What's that face for? Wipe that look off your face. It's not gross, what death is gross, it happens to everybody. I took your grandfather's bones on his two-year anniversary. We dug up his bones, we cleaned them, we carved them, and we cared for him. That's what it means, unveiling, when the body is gone, taking care of the bones, it's what we do. I did that for my father. And don't tell me times change and respect goes out the window. I want to touch. To touch his lips, to feel his breath through me to feel his sound, deep low. He's lonely you know. Why do you have to be so stubborn? What does it take, Rapai? A shovel. So what. Why do you think I whisper in your ear? Of all my children, of all my children, you've got the guts, what's there to be afraid of, dirt is dirt, bones are bones, and music is music. Come on, you know what's under that dirt, you know I'm dead. We all know. I'm bones. We both know that. So you think you keep it all buried, you never deal with remains, remains should remain hidden, remain gone, remain blocked from your eyes, because maybe if you don't see it, it never was, What you got that face on for? You think it's gross? So? Human bodies are disgusting from day one, we're disgusting all through our lives, we're disgusting, how many times I dealt with your disgusting rear end, and raised you up. What are you afraid of, Rapai? Disturbing me? Like I've got the hotel sign on, do not disturb, you're not going to disturb me, I'm not down there, that's just bones down there. You want to lock me away in a box, forget me, I live in you I live in you I'm your breath, your footsteps—

Today's the day. Remember what I told you. Before I died and became one of a long long line, of your long long line of ancestors. My face will be remembered, my bones will be carved into songs, my spirit will be carved into stories. Put your hands in the dirt. Be selfless. And dig. That's right dig. I'll sing to you. Dig. What was that song? Dig down. What was that song? I'll sing to you. Dig.

By Definition

RACHEL AXLER

HELEN is a college student.

HELEN: David. I looked it up. Do you realize that? After that conversation, it was burning a hole in my brain, and I had to find it. Well, of course, I didn't have it. I found the dictionary on the floor, torn in half—and how you managed that, I won't ask—but of course you'd taken the half that it would have been in. So I went out that night, and I went to the library and I found a whole dictionary, and I looked it up. Listen: "Love. Noun. A deep, tender, ineffable feeling of affection and solicitude toward a person, such as that arising from kinship, recognition of attractive qualities, or a sense of underlying oneness." Isn't that nice? "Underlying oneness." Nice. Or pretty, or . . .

But, see, the most important word in there comes at the beginning. "Ineffable." I looked up that one, too, just to be sure. And there it was. My reasoning, in print. "Ineffable. Adjective. Inexpressible. Too sacred to be spoken." You want to extend it, or should I? Okay, I will. By definition, I couldn't tell you that I loved you. Or by definition, my inability to do so proved my feelings beyond words. "Beyond words." Isn't that funny? All things considered, I mean. But what's funnier, and I'm not talking about ha-ha funny, is the opposite viewpoint. I mean, yours. You see, if Webster is right, and he hasn't failed me yet, your capacity for such a . . . simple and grandiose statement . . . belied your emotions. Do you get what I'm saying? David? I mean your ability to say "I love you" proved that you didn't. By definition. By . . . syllogism. There's a word. Right? I said, there's a wrecking ball of a word.

Did you ever want to disprove some fundamental formula—destroy a tenet of . . . algebra or something and throw the world of mathematics on its head?

I don't even know what I'm talking about. That about which I'm . . .

What are you thinking?

David?

The Strawberry Scene

BIANCA BAGATOURIAN

LARA wipes her eyes and sits down. A red light shines.

LARA: It was my second day at the office. He'd asked me to lunch. We connected instantly. He invited me to one of those places with red leather seats with the big buttons, you know, where the waitresses mill around in short black skirts and there's smoke everywhere and everyone's eating thick red meat.

I arrived late. We didn't really talk at first, we just kind of "looked" a lot, until the food came. I got this burger with some fruit on the side, and there was this strawberry he just kept staring at. First he told me he hated strawberries. Then he asked if he could have it . . . said he wanted it . . . had to have it . . . that it looked so all alone . . .

Perhaps it was the redness of the berry or maybe even its half-bitten form. Something about the berry gave it all away. The manner in which I had discarded it and the way in which he picked it up. His tone as he uttered "may I," my eagerness in returning "of course." The shiny attractiveness of its exterior, the bland dullness of its taste filled the moment awkwardly.

Was it the berry or that very small scene, the smallness of the gesture or the grandness of its touch? It happened so instantly and yet between the lines, above the words, beneath the moves, was it what I said or what he chose to hear, what I wanted most or what he did just need? It happened so suddenly, it was such a rush, a second, it wasn't more or maybe even less. Could it have been the momentary look, the gaze that said it all or the way the stare portrayed? It was in my eyes just as it was in his, in my mind as was in my head. On my lips, on his tongue, yet never in one sentence. In the sounds and the moves and all around us spelled that very same thought that tied us up inside and on the outside all you saw was some smoky exhalation that engulfed two people in a cloud of serene space.

If you looked at these two, undoubtedly you'd think, what a pair, what a couple to be sharing such a place.

"Are you married?" I asked. "Are you looking?" he replied. And then a long still silence pursued. "Just asking," as I turned a shade very close to that of a particular berry in mind.

I had no idea he was married.

Excerpt from *A Body of Water*

NEENA BEBER

MARGUERITE is sunbathing on a beach. She is in her late teens or late sixties, depending on whether we are flashing forward or backward in time.

MARGUERITE: I look fat. Do I look fat? Look at me. I'm so fat. This bathing suit makes me look fat. Admit it. I'm, like, total-ly bloated. I just—uchh—it's disgusting. (*Sees passerby.*) Do I look like that? I look like that, right?

(*She stands and steps forward into a different space and time.*) Years later I develop a conscience, a strong moral fiber, an interest in social justice. I march for human rights, I march against fur, I march for humanitarian efforts abroad, I march against hunger, I march for the environment, I march for Palestinians, Bosnians, Hindus, Tibetans, Sri Lankans, Peruvians, Christians, and Jews, I chain myself to a tree, to a wall, to a tractor, I am sent to prison for a short time, I am stabbed in prison, I survive, the scar gets darker over time before it fades.

(*Goes back to sunning and looks at her own teenage flesh.*) This should not be here. I'm supposed to be in the prime of my youth, the full bloom or whatever. Most people don't even have to exercise until they're way into their like twenties or something, and look at me, I'm already—I hate this. (*Observing someone else.*) Some people look really good in bathing suits and some people don't. (*To us.*) You're so skinny. I wish I were skinny like you. (*Looking toward ocean.*) There aren't even any waves today. No big ones, anyway, none you can ride. It's so calm.

(*Stepping forward in space and time.*) Years later, I find

myself at a train station after my divorce, which is bitter and protracted. I have an existential crisis. I travel widely. I come to understand my mother. (*Not knowing why.*) Years later, I cry at such simple things.

(*Stepping back, observing someone else.*) God. I hope I don't get that old. I can't imagine it. Can you imagine—us? No way. They'll probably have things they can do to keep it all together by then, right? I hate growing up in a beach community. It's a lot of pressure, you know? At this age. I liked being a little girl and not thinking about it. Little kids are perfect. And they don't have to think about it. It never comes up. They just don't.

(*Stepping forward.*) Years later I long to return to the water, to the heat, to the hard pillows of sand, to that feeling, that feeling that you get only from the ocean, and the air like this, the way it smells, the stickiness the saltiness the heat— My room is small and far from the ocean but I long to return . . : to this.

(*Back at the beach.*) Are you going in? I heard there are jelly fish, the kind that sting. I don't care, I'm going in! (*Marguerite runs towards the water.*)

Winter with Tambourine Boy

BROOKE BERMAN

LIDDY: It is January, and I am nineteen, home from my first semester at school. You are my friend from home. This is home, and you are my friend. And since my mother died, there is no one to stay with anymore, when I come home. So, I come home to you—with your big steel-tipped boots and your pierced ear and your apartment on Armitage Street, next to the El tracks.

I am here, and you are not. You are in Indiana shooting a drivers' ed training film. We call that "an industrial," we in the know. You have the lead in this industrial, which is funny since you don't know how to drive, but you're faking it O.K. for the cameras.

Now, the light in your apartment affects me in funny ways. It makes me dance around the kitchen in thermal underwear or lie on the floor under patches of sun, hoping to soak the fragmented sunlight into my skin because Chicago in January can be cruel. The light makes me color with my red and purple crayons on your lime green linoleum floor. Just for effect. The light makes me eat things I normally wouldn't eat, like chocolate milk and toast, because that's all you've got here, and for some reason I'm just too lame to go buy anything else. The light makes me steal toilet paper from the diner around the corner because you never buy any, and it makes me put the rolls of stolen toilet paper in your big Guatemalen bag and buy a cup of coffee and run. The light is making me do all of these things; it's one of those real dizzy intoxicating lights, like the light that shines off your skin and teeth and hair. And you aren't even here so this is in my memory.

You call and leave messages for me to listen to on the machine. You call every day from that motel in Indiana.

The messages go like this:

BEEP

I say, "Hey, it's me, and I'm in your apartment."

And, you say, "Make yourself at home."

And I say, "Okay. I'm gonna go out this afternoon in the fucking freezing cold, maybe to the art museum. When are you coming home? It's cold here. And what's up with your heat?"

And you say, "Use the space heater in the bedroom. It's really awesome and it's the only way to get warm at all."

And I say, "The space heater rocks my world."

And you say, "Good."

The night you come home (at last!!), you entertain me with stories about the cast and crew and the director who kept trying to get you to "ground." Neither of us knows what that means—"to ground." We conjecture, but we really don't know. I am on the floor again—or still—in your room this time, pressed up against the heater (which you were right about) with my legs shooting straight in the air, my skirt down around my ears, long johns exposed.

You come home, bringing trail mix and cheap ice cream and we eat it for dinner and tell stories of our days apart. You brought your tambourine with you to Indiana ("Maybe that's why she thought you were ungrounded," I say) and home again, and after eating all the ice cream, we pretend to be a tambourine band on the streets of your North Side neighborhood. This lasts as long as the wind chill permits, which is actually sort of long.

Now, I have gotten very good at giving out this address as my own. Do you even know how many people I give your address to? Phone number, maybe, because I know they call. But address. Sometimes even your last name. I pretend that it is mine, I don't know why, really.

A week passes. Just like this. And then a second. You're in

school now—while I'm on vacation—and I hang out around the theater building watching all the actors who you assure me will one day be famous. We take bets on which ones. And I drink lemon tea all afternoon at Java Jive and mocha lattes at Kava Kave. And I wait for you to get done and play with me.

"Let's pretend we're married," you say, like the Prince song—it is a song—and so we do. I wear a tinfoil ring for a whole three days until it falls off.

One night, late, we take a walk West, over the bridge to a cafe called Voltaire, and on the way we meet an old lady who talks to us in Spanish and puts her hand on my belly as if I am pregnant. I am certainly not pregnant, since we have never had sex, never even kissed on the mouth, although I think of both of these as valid options but just don't tell you and I don't know how to seduce. So, unless it is a virgin birth, I cannot be pregnant, though I think I would like to be—with myself. I would like to give birth. And I wonder if now, after her touch on my flat virgin belly, I will.

I am going back to California soon. That's where I go to school. And between you and me, I don't know if that is really a good idea. My brother is nearby, and I see him a lot. But Berkeley is a weird place to be if you're an eighteen-year-old girl with a dead crazy mom and a Buddhist brother and a heart somewhere else.

But for now, I'm still in Chicago with you. I'm in your blue painted shower singing songs and using your towels. I'm on your green chair eating Cheerios and chocolate milk. I'm hopping up and down on one leg and listening to all of your favorite songs from the nineteen-eighties because it is now the end of the decade and we feel we should take stock.

A month later, Valentine's Day—but that is just a coincidence—you call me at school, telling me to watch for you on some TV fast-food commercial, and so I do. You are the same. I am the same. Where are you again? Why is there this thing called distance? We are too young to know anything really about change or losing each other. Both of which will come, in the not too distant future. But we do not know about that. We are still best friends—and it doesn't even matter yet that we've never kissed. And never will.

Perry Mason, Parakeets, and Gorgonzola

MEREDITH BESSER

*A thirty-something single woman contemplates being dumped by
her most recent boyfriend.*

I'm a wonderful person.

All my boyfriends who've broken up with me say so. They
all want to be friends. They all say I've taught them a lot and
they'll never forget me. This was a typical breakup although
they all vary slightly. It went like this.

We have a date Thursday night. "Hey beautiful" is how
he greets me in a low sexy voice. We talk about a party we
plan to go to next week. We walk the short distance to the
pier and dance freely to live reggae music. We share a bottle of
Sauvignon Blanc (having decided we prefer it to
Chardonnay). He kisses me goodnight and hugs me too tight-
ly. He doesn't call me on Friday. It's the first Friday since I've
known him that he doesn't call.

I'm restless that night. I dream that my parakeet escapes,
slipping through the bars of his cage. It's summertime and the
front door's open. He heads for the door having seen blue
pieces of sky, flapping furiously (he's been confined for some
time). I race to shut the door, heaving as I grab the knob and
push with all my weight, terrified that I'll slam it on his tiny
body. That's when I wake up, sweaty and gasping for air. I sit
up in bed, way too alert. I turn on the TV for comfort, but I
don't have cable, and the only non-infomercial program at
3:30 a.m. is the middle of an old black and white Perry Mason
show. Even though it's the middle, the plot's not hard to pick

up. There's usually a fragile, pretty young woman facing trial for the atrocious murder of her lover, who deserved it for some inexcusable testosterone-driven act of cruelty. Every time I'm awake at 3:30 a.m. I watch someone tearfully confessing, driven by a guilty 1950s conscience that's been deeply stimulated by Perry Mason's skillful questioning. Perry Mason appears to be a terrific attorney. Perry Mason hasn't met the right woman yet. Perry Mason is someone I would probably date.

Why can't men be more like Perry Mason?

I live in my apartment with my parakeet (the one that appears in my dream). I found him in the public park, wandering near the pathway. A curious golden retriever on a long leash came sniffing around him. I pushed the dog out of the way and kneeled down and beckoned to the parakeet in my best parakeet-speak. He leapt into the palm of my extended hand. He was pretty motley. He acted blasé, but he had feathers that pointed in every direction and he hadn't eaten well for days. He was hungry. He didn't realize how bad off he was. So I got him a cage. A home of his own. I get tense when I think about him escaping. Or when I dream about him escaping.

The day I found him I carried the parakeet between my cupped hands to a nearby market where I bought him some birdseed and a mirror with a bright purple frame. Parakeets like to look at themselves in mirrors. They think they're in the company of another like-minded and attractive creature. In the comfort of their own cage.

Why can't men be more like parakeets?

I met my ex-boyfriends in various ways: through friends, at work, in class, on blind dates. But I might as well have found them wandering through the park, a park fraught with hidden hazards. They come to me messy and I fix them up. I let them be themselves. I worship their every transient thought. They begin to feel confident, self-assured. After several months, a year or two with me, they find better jobs, cars and homes. They make sure to thank me as they flee.

On Saturday, mid-afternoon, he calls. I can't decide if I

should pick up the phone or let him continue to leave a message on my machine and think that I'm casually out, doing important things and living my life. His voice on my machine is soft, familiar and finally irresistible, so I grab the phone before he finishes. He sounds apologetic, like a dog that's peed on the floor, as he asks to see me. Of course I agree to see him.

No man I've ever known has been able to handle fairly unconditional love. Which brings me to Gorgonzola.

He came over and sat on my couch. In the same spot he always sat. His lids were lowered and his eyes were misty. I felt oddly comforted to see him emitting moisture. It took a while until he spoke. Waiting for the words to form on his lips felt like being stabbed really slowly. About a thousand times. I imagined a scenario where he pulls out a gun, aims quickly at me and shoots. He drops the gun and scrambles out the door. It's a sultry summer day and all my neighbors are at the beach so no one hears the shot. I quickly bleed to death after having passed out. That would have been charitably painless. But that doesn't happen. Breaking up is like being tried and your boyfriend, soon to be ex, is like Perry Mason. He makes a good case, points the finger at you and doesn't allow bail to be set.

He says, "We're out of sync, we'd make better friends, we just can't communicate." I have a difficult time understanding him. "What do you mean, what's out of sync? And how can we ever be friends if we can't communicate?" I ask. He flails his hands into the air. He says nothing. "When did we get out of sync? Have we been out of sync all this time?" I continue, feeling like I'm failing some big final exam in slow motion. He just stares at me and his face turns rosy. "It's over," he says.

At that moment it becomes apparent to me that he's already discussed this, except I wasn't present. If I know him at all, which I've just been told that I don't, rehearsal took place at his therapist's Beverly Hills office a day earlier. After all, he was an actor. In L.A., rehearsal's imperative. An unprepared non-professional like me couldn't argue. We were, ladies and gentlemen of the jury, unable to communicate. I was guilty as charged.

But I stray from the Gorgonzola.

I never tasted Gorgonzola until he bought it for our Hollywood Bowl outing. We were shopping together and I told him I approved of his choice. It's one of those lies told to your lover when you're too busy swooning to care about details. I always ate those benign cheeses with names like cheddar, cottage and cream.

So even though I'd been sentenced to ponder my inadequacies as a girlfriend (with only a slight chance of probation), there was some good news.

I ate the Gorgonzola.

I discovered that I love Gorgonzola. It tastes surprising, yet familiar. It darts around the mouth and the tangy flavor stays with you. It's soft and crumbly, vulnerable and forgiving, yet has the wisdom of a harder cheese twice its age.

Why can't men be more like Gorgonzola?

The moment I shut the door and listened to the vague squeak of his designer sneakers bolting down the steps of my apartment building, I went to the fridge and cut off a chunk of Gorgonzola with my biggest, sharpest kitchen knife, the one generally reserved for cutting up chickens. I placed a piece of Gorgonzola on my tongue. It had little craters and felt slippery. I sucked on it like a gumball. I couldn't have been more satisfied. Well, I guess I could have. But Gorgonzola was kinda fun. I'll always have Gorgonzola.

And, there's the company of my parakeet, who seems to have learned to accept fairly unconditional love without a great deal of angst. In honor of the breakup, I bought him a hanging four-sided mirror with an attached shiny silver bell.

As he tweaked his bell and admired his fluffy green image in all four sides of his new mirror, I retraced the details of my breakup. He listened politely, his bell chiming in agreement. After I finished, I informed him that cooler weather was approaching, and that, in case he was concerned, I'd be keeping the front door shut.

The Women of Lockerbie

DEBORAH BREVOORT

MADELINE LIVINGSTON (late 40–50s), whose only son Adam was killed in the crash of Pan Am 103 over Lockerbie Scotland, has come to Lockerbie on the seventh anniversary of the crash. Still overcome with grief, she is roaming the hills looking for her son's remains, which were never found. She meets the women of the village and tells them of the moment she got the news.

MADELINE:
I was in the kitchen.
I was baking a pie for Adam.
A pumpkin pie
to welcome him home.
The TV was on.
I listen to it when I'm cooking.
It was tuned to a soap opera.
"All my Children."
One of the couples was fighting.
The woman was pregnant.
She wanted to get an abortion.
"Don't be a fool!" I say to the woman. "Have the baby!"
I sprinkle flour on the counter and roll out the pie dough.
I roll it once in each direction.
Like this . . .
(*She rolls.*)
The way my mother taught me.
And then Ted Koppel comes on the air.
I know immediately that something is wrong.
You only hear Ted Koppel's voice at night
never in the day.

He said:
"We interrupt this program . . ."
I thought,
"Oh dear,
Something awful has happened.
What a shame. And so close to Christmas."
I grab more flour and sprinkle it.
I roll the crust.
I hear . . .
"Pan Am 103."
The pie dough sticks to the rolling pin.
"Pan Am 103 was last seen in a fireball over Scotland."
I double over.
I sink onto the kitchen counter.
My face presses into the pie dough.
It is cold on my nose and cheek.
I cannot stand up.
I grope the counter for something to hold on to.
My arm hits the flour bin.
It crashes to the floor.
My feet are covered with flour.
I reach for the handle on the refrigerator.
I pull myself up.
And there
in front of me
is a note
held by a magnet
that says
"Adam. 7 p.m. JFK. Pan Am 103."

Excerpt from *con flama*

SHARON BRIDGFORTH

GRANDMOTHER is from the deep south.

GRANDMOTHER:
i have always had what you call a
special
way with numbers.
every set every order every combination that i have ever heard
        or laid eyes on is still in my head
just as fresh as when it first got there.
that's why they calls me count
cause if a number is involved
you can
count
on me.

and i must say
numbers have been very very good to me.
i gots a pile of fives under my mattress a stack of tens buried
        in the backyard
and i done had enough twenties to buy my home and them
        buildings where i keeps my assets and things
    which i encourage all the peoples to get theyselves some
        assets
    cause when yo ass get old/you best have somewhere to set
yessuh
so, when the young peoples asked
if they could use my establishments and things for they meeting
i said
why sho

come on in.
and when i heard that they was planning to burn down the
          buildings that housed the relentless and cruel business
          doers of this here fine community
i said
children your plan sounds good
the only thing is
you done forgot about the numbers. but don't you worry
          none
cause i am here to help you get hold to
the numbers.

so, as planned
different disbatches would pile up in they little ole cars
pull up yelling and breaking windows
toss a little fire through
drive off.
the police and the firemens would come a running place to
          place
always just a little too late.
meanwhile
me and lil naynay would get
into
a certain place
cause you know a little Coloured gal and a old Coloured
          woman be the last thing
any body
be paying attention to
well we'd find all the records of debt them businesses had
          forced on our fine community members
and we destroyed them numbers!

we made it to every furniture store department store grocery
          store for miles
cept we left mr. rosenbaum's and mr. chung's places alone
          cause they have been long upstanding examples of

humanity towards the peoples/and of course we didn't
bother the Coloured businesses but except that got-
dang ole mr. johnson and his lecherous self loathing
oreo ass liquor store
his records burned baby   ha!

well
we had to retire that next evening cause the highway patrol
        and national guards had done declared war on watts
and it wasn't safe for no Coloured be to nowhere
not even in your own home really.
but
the victory was already ours
see our group
we didn't harm no peoples
and we didn't touch or destroy not one library church home
        or fair run business
but we got the numbers of the ruthless baby
we hurt them in they numbers
and you know that in this here u. s. of a.
everything
have always
been about the numbers.
ha!

I Am Not a Black Woman

KIM BRUNDIDGE

The MOTHER, in her 40s, has just had yet another big argument with her teenage son.

MOTHER: I am not a black woman. (*Beat*) I'm not. You know who I'm talking about. That wide-hipped, big-assed, brown-skinned powerhouse who takes no shit off of anybody. Nobody. Not her man. Not her enemies. Definitely not her kids. (*Beat*) Nope, I'm not her. (*Beat*) I thought I was. Lord knows, I tried to be. Thought she ran in my family. Thought she was my mama's mama and her mama's mama. Thought she was an inherent unquestioned particle in my DNA. A given. Well, I tell you what, if she runs in my family, she ran straight past me. (*Beat*) I'm not supposed to admit it, I know, not even to myself. But I have to. Cuz I can't sell it anymore. Not like I used to. Used to sell it, from early on. Sure did. Sold it at a *discount*. To my man. To my kids. Everybody. I'm pretty sure my daughter bought it. She's selling it, too, now. Like Amway. My son even bought in, at one point. Thought I was the beginning and the end. The end all and be all. Just like he's s'posed to think. "Home is wherever you are, mama." That what he told me when I asked him how he felt about moving across country. Used to crawl up on the sofa with me and watch TV. Real comfortable. For a long time. Till he didn't anymore. Till he found out I wasn't legit. Till he couldn't forgive me. Yep, at one point, he thought his mama was a *black woman*. But he found me out. And he just couldn't forgive me for not being that *rock*, that solid mound of granite he could stand behind and be safe, protected from the world. No matter what. See, he wanted me to put on my cape (*she puts the apron around her shoulders*) and defend him from the enemy (*her weapon is a big spoon or a small frying pan*) with the strength and all the spirit of all the other black women in my genes. Protect him from the enemy, whoever and whatever the enemy was. Protect him from the predators that prey on little boys. Child molesters and angry men of God and nightmares and big fat hungry roaches. *Mommy! Mommy! Get it, Mommy. Get it!!* That's what he wanted. He wanted me to keep him safe. But I didn't. Cuz I couldn't. (*Beat*) So he fired me. (*Several beats*) I tried. I tried my best to hold up my half of the sky. I didn't make collard greens, I made stir fry. And I didn't fry chicken. I fried tofu. And I didn't make him drink milk cuz I never liked it either. And I let him have his say cuz I felt like I never had mine. But I got tired. Tired of being mama and daddy. Tired of working like a man and crying like a woman. Tired of patching up fuming holes in my living room walls and explaining to well-meaning teachers that he was talkative and restless because he was *bored* not because he was a problem child. I got tired. (*Beat*) I should have beat his ass. That's what they kept telling me. All you gotta do is beat his ass. That'll get him straight. Right. But I couldn't. "You're afraid of him." That's what people kept saying. But it wasn't that. (*Beat*) I didn't have her in me. That no-nonsense black woman. That woman who goes into survival mode when somebody, *anybody* threatens her. She didn't kick in when his spit sprayed my face or when he put his strong, furious body in the doorway so I couldn't leave the room. (*Beat*) I was afraid *for* him. That he had lost his mind. That some relentless demon had taken possession of his soul last night in his sleep or that afternoon in fifth period. *That* I was afraid of.

Excerpt from *Kate Crackernuts*

SHEILA CALLAGHAN

KATE'S MOTHER, a 40-ish fading beauty, is tending to her garden.

KATE'S MOTHER: He tasted like the sun and he would slip-slide into me and I wore summer dresses with thin straps and he'd break them right off with his complexion and his wife ha she was a glob of mayonnaise at the side of his mouth and I just wiped her away and sometimes I got scared that might be me someday but then my straps would break and I was wind again and even though his daughter was honey-lovely and you, Kate, were a powdery scone he took me, he took us both, we were minty and we gleamed in his home like two freshly brushed front teeth but now we've drained through the floorboards and I am less than a name, I'm a condiment I am a symbol of nothing and he doesn't see me and maybe I could make something happen and maybe I could pull a fat rainbow of kitsch from my womb and tie it in a bow around his head but right now he doesn't see me, see me you bastard, I am an orchid I am a glass of milk I could be anything . . . anything.

Excerpt from *Scab*

SHEILA CALLAGHAN

ANIMA, a 23-year-old woman, in a bar is very drunk.

ANIMA: What a piece of work is man, how noble in reason, how infinite in faculty, in form and move and inespresso ada-mahble . . . That's Shakespeare. I know more. I played Hamlet once in college. It was for a video project but I was good. No one could believe a chick Hamlet could be so goddamn good.

Why not? Men played women's roles for years and years and years, no one had a problem. I made people CRY. Because I could *hear* them, assface. Sniff-sniff from behind me, honking into a hanky in front of me, wet gurgling noises on my right . . . That's a fucked-up feeling, you know? People who don't even know you, they believe so hard in your lie they make it their own.

I'm not going to tell you my fucking name. I'm not here to get hit on. I'm just having a cocktail. (*She drinks.*) An actor, really? Quite a rarity in these parts. No, I don't act anymore. I study. Eighteenth-century theatre. No, Shakespeare was earli-er. No, Tennessee Williams was later. No, Galileo was an astronomer. It's okay, everyone gets them mixed up.

Excerpt from *Braille Garden*

DARRAH CLOUD

GRACE is a WASP alcoholic in her 50s.

GRACE: It's after five o'clock! I need a drink! (*She accepts a drink. Stares at it.*) You know I can't drink out of a bottle, Gus. I need a glass! Please get me a glass!

I make everything difficult, don't I? I'm so sorry. I don't mean to . . . Need never changes. Don't you understand? Nothing ever changes. (*She sips her drink.*)

I didn't used to be like this. . . . I was a dancer once. Did you know that? I trained all my young life in a room without heat . . . with only a mirror to teach me, and a man from a failed ballet. . . . One day I remember, spring was too much to contain, and Teacher took us to the ocean, hours away. There I danced in a dress like fog at the edge of the Atlantic, on the sand. . . . I leapt higher than I'd ever leapt before . . . and everyone was amazed. No one knew how I could do it. It was because I trusted the sand. I knew I would come down, you see. You can go very high when you're sure of what's beneath you. . . . But then, a man with a camera came suddenly by . . . And he froze me there, froze me in mid-air . . . and I never came down after that. He got very famous for it. And I've been stuck in the air ever since.

So Far

CONSTANCE CONGDON

RAINY, a young girl, is talking to her android companion. They are in a post-apocalyptic world run by a Matriarch, her mother.

So how I was born, come to be, that is the question? It were a dark and stormy night—really, it was—and Mama wanted to be with child bad. She loved the throwing up with the sun-rise—it were a way to cover up the hangover. She loved being fat with no questions asked. She loved having a reason to not do or think but just to be. Action had been her lover and her undoing. Trying to prove that she could be King. It were hard and I appreciate that. So she worked me dad up and then said, "I can't stand ye. I'll be in my quarters." So me dad did what he could and put it in his helmet—we was at war, of course—and left it outside her tent. Then it rained, but warm rain, and the little mud doggies kept swimming. Me dad wanted me to be born, so he sent mom a telepathetic message—"look for me outside." Well, Mama always paid more attention to messages in her own head than anything she got through her ears. So she rose up from her bed where she had been pining, so she says, for the loss of her love of me dad, and the potential of having his seed so that all the children will be matched, like some ammunition won't fit in some guns but in others it will. She poked her head out the tent flap to find the helmet—knew immediately what it was and administered it to herself with a funnel she made from a map of the countryside with current troop movements in red. Consequently, my complexion was quite pink, but I was called Rainy on account of half of me lived for a while in warm rain before I was sliding, wild, toward the big, white planet that was my Home and then my Self.

Addicts

TÖNYA DERRICKSON

MONA is an aged, yet ageless, homeless woman on a bench, talking to herself or anyone around her.

MONA: It's happening. You see it on the news, TV, radio, paper. It's all over. Kids blowing away kids . . . in schools . . . man that shit never used to happen . . . never carried more'n pocketknife . . . maybe a hunting knife . . . but definitely no *guns* in schools . . . but now . . . now! Kids these days! . . . twelve-year-old 007s. Rats, I'm telling you—they are all rats. . . . You know what happens to rats right? When you put'm together? In a cage that isn't big enough and they multiply . . . and multiply. . . . They go crazy. Any dime store psychologist will tell you that. Eat each other—literally. And incest . . . and infanticide. Every sort of deviant behavior. Babies start having babies . . . smothering them during prom . . . throwing them off Lover's Bluff . . . where it all starts anyway in the back of Daddy's car, pumping between her thighs better than any ol'*touch*down against Central High. Ought'a cut 'em back . . . fucking kids . . . and my kid. My son . . . says there ain't no such person as Hitler . . . it was a media hype. Fucking media hype!

Maybe we shouldn't start pruning the kids . . . maybe we should start with the teachers . . . what do they think they teach these days! Media hype my ass. Oh I know who you are—I know who's teaching now days! The goddamn little prick who got to go to the U on a swimming scholarship, that's who! Full goddamn tuition paid while I worked my goddamn ass off to put myself through college . . . yeah, don't help the "straight-A" bio major, help the jackass she has to tutor. Help the fucking "C" student who can swim (but not good enough for the Olympics) who wakes up from his alcoholic stupor long enough to realize that *companies don't hire professional SWIMMERS* so he cuts a fucking teaching certificate and gets a job at your local district teaching PE and THEN, because they are *short handed* they let him teach *GEOGRAPHY*, and *MATH* and *HISTORY* that makes Hitler just a media hype! Cuz now, that swimmer's in *The System.* And *The System* says that they'll build a *multi-million dollar stadium* but they're too GODDAMN CHEAP TO PAY FOR A *DECENT FUCKING TEACHER!*

(*Pause*)

Have you ever felt this black rage twist your bowels, billowing inside you until you feel so powerful yet so helpless that all you want to do is bloody your hands against whatever brought you here? (*Pause*) Yeah. Me neither. But it's coming. The world is exploding with "C" students in their stupors, breeding babies and there's nowhere for them to go 'cept crowd in their cages, work their nine to fives, exist in their sorry ass routines. Minds lulled and dulled to the point where only the "most shocking" and "most outrageous" becomes enough to break through their pathetic commonplace lives. *Those* are the interbred less-than-humans hungering for attention . . . *Look at me . . . look at me . . . look at me.* . . . Cuz let's face it . . . kids shooting kids is passé. Now we just shake our collective heads . . . "Tsk tsk tsk . . . kids these days." But they aren't kids anymore are they? They're the offspring of the less-than-humans. They're rats. Rats with rage.

Circles

CONSTANCE DIAL

This business of love and romance is a laugh. The last few years when our bed was no more than a place to rest . . . sleep was impossible. He'd lie there on his back, sometimes all night, staring at the ceiling. (*She puts the pillow in his place and moves closer to it.*) He was awake, dreaming. He'd rub his hand over his chest and I could see his angry fist tighten. (*Whispers.*) Say it, Tom. I'd be screaming inside. Tell me how it aches. He never did of course. He'd wet the bed, hide from me all morning, the fool, proud as an ass all his life. Never touched another woman, except Susan. He went to her twice. When the first baby died he went to Susan. He couldn't bear to touch me then. It was as if I hurt him. It wasn't the same. He told me there was coldness in their lovemaking. He came back to our games. He wanted her again when he first got sick. (*Laughs.*) But he blubbered all over the bed and she sent him home again. After that night he stayed with me until he died. He died in his sleep. Never said goodbye, goodnight . . . not a word, just died. (*Slips out of her robe, lies with her shoulder touching the pillow.*) The coldness from his body sent a chill through me in the dark. (*Sits up.*) I turned up the light and he was gone. I studied him for hours. All night, I think. Those pale blue eyes looked surprised, confused. His fist was clenched so tight I couldn't move it. The blood had settled from his face. He looked like a marble statue, someone's best work of a foolish, dead, old man. Still, I didn't enjoy the thought of never seeing him again. I touched his face, the way he never allowed when his head could turn away. I defiled his body that night. Told him things I had hidden forty years, talked about feelings and babies and his stubborn, foolish pride. I uncovered him and lay beside the dead flesh. I whispered a lifetime of sorrow into an empty tomb. In the morning, death had stained that perfect stone. I sat in bed and watched the gray lines tint his chin, work slowly up his thighs. I watched him and thought how lucky he was to have someone with him. He wasn't closed up in a black box by himself. He was lying in his own bed while I watched death cover him as gently as a mother covers her first born. On the second day, or whenever it was, my son disturbed us. He came and took Tom away. He gave me something and I slept a long time. He had more to show me. I'm certain. Now, sometimes at night when I'm alone I put this pillow on his side of the bed. I lay beside him on my back. I close my eyes and pretend we're talking like that last night. (*She puts on her robe, sits in the rocker.*) It's too bad he wouldn't have allowed that every so often . . . maybe Susan wouldn't . . . oh well. That's silly. The old fool's dead now and the point is . . . I'm not quite sure what the point is any more.

The Four Effs

DONNA DINOVELLI

I walk into a classroom. There is no teacher present. Across the blackboard in large chalk letters are the words: Name the Four F's. Everyone else is already seated: paper and pencil poised. I am confused. Did I forget to study for this quiz? And what subject is this? A geography question? (I can't get beyond Finland, France, Fiji . . .) Language arts? (All I can think of is the word, *infinitive*.)

Then I notice all the boys are laughing and poking each other in the ribs. Jean Marie Agnold gets up—except now she's Connie Francis—and erases the board. The boys throw pencils at her. She hides under the teacher's desk.

I look at the boys and think: "FFFFFFF . . . Fart!"

At the count of three, all the boys grab a girl. Walter Donovan grabs my arm because he gave me his lucky rabbit foot two weeks ago and so considers me his girlfriend. All the boys laugh as they try to whisper the answer to the girl of their choice. They end up yelling:

"Find 'em.

Feel 'em.

Fuck 'em.

Forget 'em."

I run home.

Home is a long way away and as I run, I notice Walter Donovan running after me. No one is on the street, and it is suddenly night. Roots on the path trip me. I get up and run with Walter on my heels making "eff" sounds with his mouth. I make it to the house, slam the door, and scramble up the stairs to our second floor apartment. I run into the kitchen out of breath and begin pulling down all the window shades.

My mother is washing dishes and notices Walter outside staring up at her.

"Oh, look," she says. "Walter Donovan. Why don't you ask him in?"

F2F

LINDA EISENSTEIN

HELENA is middle-aged or more, and feeling every year of it. She might be hunched over a computer laptop, her face bathed in the eerie blue light of the screen.

HELENA: You ever have an F2F? In Internet-speak that's a Face-to-Face: that first meeting with somebody you've connected with through email or an on-line chat room. It's one of the main oddities of doing business on the 'Net, that you usually don't have a clue what somebody is going to look like, unless they've sent you a picture. You can be utterly off-base about their age, race, looks, size—sometimes even their gender. Which is what makes the F2F so revelatory. Oh, not about them. About yourself, and your expectations, the way you imagine people to be.

Well, I travel a lot so I've done a lot of them. I make a conscious effort to meet people over a cup of coffee and chat them up if I've liked them on-line. What I've discovered is that in most F2F's there's this little blip of adjustment while you revise your mental photo, but usually no huge surprises, and even if there are, you can recover in a minute or two.

Usually. Until the afternoon I look up from the menu in a cafe in a Sunbelt city and the physical reality of Trudy knocks me half out of my head. Trudy. Funny how even from a name, you form a picture. The one I'd been carrying around was of this hearty middle-aged feminist colleague, the one with the sensible salt-and-pepper wash-n-wear 'do. Nope. Instead there's an awkward shock—when I realize that all this time, through all the months of networking and info-sharing, I'd been talking to this extraordinarily beautiful girl. All right, not a girl, exactly, but oh so heartbreakingly lovely, young enough to have a white neck like a swan's and a tumble of copper curls and creamy perfect white shoulders out of a Pre-Rafaelite painting.

But hey, I'm a pro. On most days I can do the schmooze with the best of 'em, after so many years the performance is almost second nature. So I gulp, carefully rearrange my face into a professional but sisterly smile, and shift into Standard Networking Mode.

And off we go, talking as usual about agents and contacts, festivals and conferences, doing the Name-Swap Tango—but for some reason, I can feel wires crossing. My words are getting all scrambled in my mouth. They're piling up like a traffic jam, because my eyes keep drifting over to her neck, the line of her shoulders and throat. It's summer and she's wearing a strapless top, not a particularly sexy or revealing one, but nevertheless in it she seems to be nothing BUT shoulders, they're looming at me across the table like the White Mountains.

I feel like a jerk, like one of those gawking construction apes who can't keep his mind on a friendly conversation because he's staring at a woman's tits, not her face. And I wonder whether she can see my eyes tracing the curve of her neck.

So I try to get back on track—blah blah contracts oh yes that publisher ba-dang ba-dang—but her neck keeps arching and it keeps getting more and more beautiful the longer I stare. I push on, and that's a mistake. See, when I get nervous I always get louder. And more blunt, more full of opinions, oh how the opinions come crashing out of me like ocean waves battering against a white sea cliff, until I am hopelessly self-conscious about this as well.

And for a moment I think: what if I just stop, interrupt, apologize and say—"Sorry. I didn't hear the last eight sentences you said because your shoulders have got me addled." But I have learned from experience that this is the kind of thing you don't say to straight women, no matter what kind of feminists they think they are. For one thing you don't want them knocking over their latte on you, as they dart for the door. And she knows too many of the people I know, I can't stand the gossipy awfulness of such an admission, the scalding hunger of it. Because frankly there's something pathetic about the way I feel in the presence of her shoulders. They make me feel hulking and ungainly and vulnerable, not to mention grayer than Methuselah, so I don't bring it up.

Instead I sip at my cappuccino—well, more like gulp at it, trying not to spill the whipped cream all over the shelf of my own breasts, but of course when I get flustered I do. So now I look like a sloppy idiot, a loud sloppy opinionated idiot, one who can't even manage a simple conversation, who is only capable of relentless ranting monologue.

So I try another tack. I start asking her questions, and as she answers, a bit shyly, I try in vain to look other places. My eyes are darting around the room, I'm looking at the crack in the faux adobe wall and the wrought iron chairs and the prices of the drinks on the menu, I'm shifting about in my chair trying to get something, ANYTHING, in the range of my vision that does not include the overwhelming sight of these shoulders.

And she gets this worried-sad look in her brown doe-like eyes, one I can suddenly read like a thought balloon floating over her head: "She thinks I'm boring." Hooboy! Of course I don't think she's boring, actually I want to hear about her work and her aspirations and I'd even listen to her talk about her boyfriend for crying out loud, if only I could stop looking at her shoulders!

So I try to imagine a giant STOP! sign hanging around her neck, but that only makes things worse. All I can see then is all the women whose necks I never touched, a long line of swans like the chorus in Swan Lake, all dancing away from me. But then I think, get a grip, you don't really want this woman, even though her heart-shaped face and Botticelli curls are pretty spectacular, what would I do with her at this point in my life anyway. All we both want is a friendly chat and an exchange of information about contacts, and I'll bet she's gotten plenty of them, she's certainly gotten more than a FEW things in her young life because of those curls and neck and all, no wonder her stuff is in print already, says a green-eyed demon in me.

I am suddenly stupefied by the ugly turn of my thoughts. And I wonder about a woman's beauty, and how in the fairy tales it is so often a black magic gift, like a poisoned apple or a face that turns people to stone. Maybe it gets in her way as much as it helps. Maybe hardly anybody will do her work because her face and neck and shoulders stops them cold. They begin to think of her as an object of beauty instead of a voice, and it's her voice she wants people to hear.

And then I understood, for the first time in my life, why some Muslim women might not be lying when they say they love the veil. And why we sit at our computers, hour after hour, peering at each other through those glowing blank screens— like clairvoyants scrying in a mirror, or a basin of water. We hear each other's voices so much more clearly that way.

And though I didn't regret this F2F, I could sense that we'd both be relieved when it was over. That we'd look forward to feeling our shapes recede and melt into those electronic mists—'til we could meet again, safe—on that blind, shimmering shore.

Lightning

ANNIE EVANS

PEGGY is wearing a terry cloth robe. She looks at the audience a long moment before she speaks.

PEGGY: Do you hate liars? How about lying? Hell, you might think it's loads of fun. But do you think it's wrong? That Peter is up there with a list, like Santa. "Remember when you said you ate your peas in '74 but you really rolled them into your napkin and stuck them behind the dog's collar?" If Simon knew what I was up to, well, he'd divorce me. And I don't want that. I don't. He's the love of my life. Not everyone can say that about their spouses. Right now, I keep imagining God striking me dead with a lightning bolt. Yes, I have a very punishing view of God, but still, don't you sometimes think there's some massive father up there with a huge foot ready to just step on you from on high? Especially when you lie? I do. Remember your first big whopper? I was six and I was in love with Richard. Richard something. He had big, brown eyes and lived in the new developments. I always stayed after school to wait for my Mom, she was an Assistant Principal. So, one afternoon, I snuck back into my classroom, turned on the lights and rearranged the desks so I was sitting next to Richard. My therapist calls this my passive-aggressive nature. Anyway, the next morning, I was happily sitting next to Richard. Lisa, who *had* been very happily sitting next to Richard, was now in the back of the room. She stood up and accused me of moving her desk. "No Lisa, I didn't move your desk." "Liar!" she cried pointing her wee little finger. "God is going to strike you dead with a lightning bolt!" (*Looks up briefly.*) Miss Dietz moved the desks back and I was left imagining an old man on a cloud about to sizzle me because I wanted Richard Something. (*Pause*) Simon hates liars. He's a bit older than me, didn't go to college right away, was a contractor in Alaska, cleaned sea otters after Exxon Valdez. Finally, he came back, got a degree in social work. I lied to him about being a virgin. I don't know why. Virginity was being highly discouraged by then. Maybe deep down I had this strange idea he wouldn't marry me, 'cause I knew right away I wanted him, like I knew I wanted Richard Something. Only, I'd been plucked a year earlier. Maybe I didn't think it counted because it was so god awful, a fumbling bumbling after an outdoor concert. He came after one thrust. Simon went with me to the University Infirmary. I got fitted for my trusty diaphragm. (*She takes a diaphragm out of her pocket.*) I still use one. I can't take hormones. They make me cry incessantly. Isn't it pretty? A simple dome. A cervical fortress. It took me forty-five minutes to get it in the first time. I shot it across the bathroom, into the toilet. Every time I'd wash it off, carefully reapply the cream, squeeze the ends and it would squirm around in my fingers like a giggly girl, then cannonball itself into the tiles. Simon finally knocked on the bathroom door. "Do you need any help?" So, *he* tried and shot it so far across the room it stuck on the opposite wall. Finally, we did some mushrooms and just watched it hang there. (*She holds the diaphragm away from her and looks at it.*) At one moment, I swear I saw it turn into the face of a child. It wasn't scary at all. It was beautiful. If I squint my eyes, I can still see her. I still see her. (*Lowers the diaphragm.*) It was Simon's idea, Simon's decision, not to have children. Our pre-nuptial agreement. I said yes to him, I agreed to the pre-nuptial on Fourth of July. A whole bunch of us were as close as they would let us bearing lawn chairs, and we had some very bad Wild Turkey, wow, that's an oxymoron. Anyway, we were the excuse for little kids to waddle down closer to the action. Simon was so cute with them. He'd make these kids belly laugh and I wanted to shout "I sleep with that man—whenever we can get my diaphragm in." I don't think they ever figured out what exactly happened, but one of the fireworks misfired, making the trajectory about 20 feet over the lawn chairs. This thing explodes, fire, ash, drop like napalm. Suddenly it was a war zone. Simon dives for these kids like a Green Beret, had those babies ducking and covering . . . and I was so filled with such an overwhelming love, I stood there like a . . . dummy. But I saw his instincts at work, and I said yes. (*Parts her hair and points.*) My head got some hot ash on it, see right here, a little scar. My red badge of love. About the closest I've ever come to being struck by lightning. Until now. Because now I'm going to tell a very big lie. And only you God. (*Holds up diaphragm and squints.*) And her. (*Pulls a pin out of her robe.*) And this pin, will know the truth. I could make an excuse, say I'm speaking for *her*, who I'm seeing in everything now. The computer screen. The melons in the store. Simon's eyes. (*Ironic*) Oh! Did I tell you? Today's my birthday. Forty. Know what he said he'd do for my birthday? A vasectomy. "Should have done it years ago." (*She holds up the diaphragm looks at it.*) So it's now or never. A good lie, or a bad lie? I'm ovulating, according to my Basil thermometer. (*Bows her head, prays.*) Dear God, I put this in your hands. I know what I'm doing. If you're going to strike me down. If I lose it all. Please . . . Thy will be done. Amen. (*She takes the pin and sticks a hole in it. She stops, looks up. After a beat, she makes several more holes in the diaphragm. She inspects her work in the light.*) And if you aren't an acid flashback, and are meant to be, I promise I will do it differently. (*She moves as if she's going to be putting in the diaphragm.*) Oh—I better put some of the jelly on. He can feel it sometimes, like a squishy trampoline, he says. (*She takes out some spermicide from her pocket. She carefully on the very top makes a little cake swirl of gel.*) Not too much. Give the fates an equal opportunity. (*She holds it up for inspection, laughs.*) Looks like a cake. . . . Happy Birthday to us. Happy Birthday to us. Happy Birthday, dear . . . Happy birthday. (*She stares at the decorated diaphragm.*)

Take Back the Classroom

NELL GRANTHAM

TEACHER is sitting at a desk, with an apple on the corner, correcting papers with a red pen.

TEACHER: There is no "Q" in biscuit. There are not 2 Ks. Hell, there aren't ANY Ks in reconcile. (*Sighs, removes flask from purse, takes a drink, speaks to audience.*) I'm a teacher. I teach. In a public school. In Virginia. 6th Grade. For 13 years. It isn't glamorous, and I'm certainly not in it for the money. And the next person who asks me why I keep coming back might just get a piece of my mind!

(*Picking up apple.*) This? No, I bring this. Every day. Kind of a metaphor I cling to, I guess. To be honest, if any of the monsters in my class brought me an apple, I'd be checking for a razor blade. I can't believe I called them monsters. They're not all bad. Really.

(*Resigned.*) It wasn't always like this. I wasn't always like this. At first I felt really good about being a teacher. It was an honorable profession. And I gained the respect of those I respected for going into the field. It took me a while to realize that all of them were teachers too. I still know a couple of them. But we don't talk much anymore. I think they feel kind of guilty for luring me into teaching. It wasn't always so bad.

And still sometimes there are good days. Days when you see a light bulb go off. Or a shy kid finally speaks up in class. Or a bully writes a poem that gives you hope. Some days are good. . . . Once in while.

Some of the teachers do okay. Their spouses or significant others—don't give me that look—if you have a problem with gay teachers I don't even want to talk to you. Anyway, some of them do okay. Two-income households. They can make it, and they can be true to the ideals that lured us all in. Honorable profession. Joy of learning. Inspiration of youth. Blah fucking blah.

I shouldn't say that. Some of them are very good, and very supportive. They bring in boxes of markers and chalk when we run out, on their own dime. They keep the rest of us on track—eyes on the prize and all that. It's the ones who stick their heads in the sand that really piss me off. Bragging about their luxurious summer vacations in exotic places while the rest of us are moonlighting at Kinko's or worse—serving bagels to our students at the Bagel Shop. I might not have been a hottie, but I had my chances. But I chose this.

I should really get out. Get out and take a job, something different. Telemarketer, stockbroker, retail, whatever. I'm pretty articulate. I can do math. And I sure as hell know how to spell. Still, it'd be so hard to start over. This is who I am. This is what I do. What else do I know? Besides, it's not just about me. It's about the kids. If I leave, who will look after the children? Mostly I stay for them.

Excerpt from *Jimmy Carter Was a Democrat*

RINNE GROFF

EMILY is an air traffic controller, and sometime Professional Air Traffic Controllers Organization activist. She's in her early 30s.

EMILY: There's a lot of pressure, a lot of pressures, a lot of forces that conspire to keep us down.

Gravity is the worst, of all those forces. You can't get away from it. Gravity's always there. It dooms us straight from the start. I read somewhere that when a woman gets pregnant, you know egg and sperm, right away that little package starts turning and stuff, and it's all affected by gravity. I mean, even before we know who we are, even before we're born; this shit, it's just pulling on us. It colors everything. What's the first thing that pops into your head when you hear these words: Up? High? She's flying? Those ought to be nice words, great words, words of potential. But on account of gravity, all you can think of is the inevitable Down, Low, She's crashed.

But then there's airplanes, right? And you watch them and you think they've really got it figured out. When a plane's taking off and there it goes gliding upwards, or if you're riding in one of those new jets, so smooth, if you have good pilot, you could maybe forget about your morbid visions of tailpipes in flames and really believe, believe for a moment that you can overcome—fuck, you could overcome anything, you're flying, you did it.

Why can't that be the way we think? Why can't we teach our children that in the womb? Not to be afraid. Not to assume yeah, sure you're Up now, but here comes Failure, you might as well throw in the towel. And if a baby could feel all right, up in the air, in a plane, soaring along, could experience freedom from all that pulls her down; if she could learn that, can't you maybe imagine that she could get free of a bunch of other shit, too? That we'd grow as a species and triumph? And change, and growth, and all that are possible?

She's flying. She's flying.

Intimate Lay

ELLEN HAGAN

A young woman speaks from the bedroom after she has let some man go.

I know the intimate lay of the sheets after they have been torn into, after the empty wet of the mouth has left stains, after the sheets are crumbled like a tangle of legs, after his smell stays, cookie-crumbs, a dirty sock, his blue sweater. After the presence of his has altered the shape of my room so that his mess is scattered around me like fingers locking into someone's hair. I kick him out and feel good. He is too preppy for me anyway. He's into stocks. He's into hair gel. He's into himself. So I open the door, his ass, the soft ball of my foot. I'll never call I want to shout. I'll block all your calls. When I have enough quarters I'll wash your smell out from my sheets. On my way for bagels this morning I saw a dead pigeon. It made me think of my desire for you. You are not welcome here anymore.

That night I made popcorn. I watched one movie, showered and put on a pair of my mother's old cotton underwear. Every girl that I know; every girl worth her weight as a daughter has borrowed a pair from her mother. Stashed in her drawer, they're the last pair she'll wear, the haven't-done-laundry pair, the I'm-not-making-love-to-anyone-soon pair. They are the most comfortable pair; the ones that make you feel earthy and grounded. My mother's underwear is soft, smooth against my skin. I am closer to her when I wear them, the womb, closer to her physical body and I love that. That night I put them on happily, slid one leg in and then the other. I didn't go out. It rained so hard and I didn't feel like getting wet.

Excerpt from *Do You Have Time to Die?*

IMANI HARRINGTON

DELPHINIA, an African American woman in her early 20s, pregnant and diagnosed with AIDS, has been arrested and sent to a penal colony. She claims her innocence to her investigating agent, Swagger, but right now she is extremely upset with how she has been treated.

DELPHINIA: Yeah, you're right, you have the papers, the files, and you have access to my information and my blood, and that's all you care about is those damn papers and what happened in the cell block. Do you know how many papers I signed before I came in here? Do you know how many pills they offered me? No, you don't. Half the time I can't see clearly and other times I can't remember. How could I when I sometimes can't even think long enough to know where I'm goin or hold somethin in my hand without droppin it. I can't take any of that medication even if I wanted to and you want information, or do you want what I have? You want this? (*Bullying Swagger, she nearly gets into her face, but quickly pulls back.*) No, you don't want what I have; they don't want what I have. But they *say* they want my blood for a cure? No more blood, no more tests and no more messin with my head. I'm sick and tired of em wantin somethin from me. You'd think by now they would have a damn cure with all the blood I gave em, all the energy I've given em, but there's still no cure. (*Beat*) I walk through those corridors every day and every health agent and guard I see wants somethin from me but nobody has any answers. Except to tell me that I'm a suicidal murderer, too anxious, too emotional, too impulsive, too irrational and that I live my life like a tramp *and* that I'm killin my child. Well, I haven't had it yet to kill it. If I am killin my child, what the hell are they doing to me? WHAT ABOUT ME!? (*Jumps in front of Swagger.*) My lover is dead, my family is dead, people are dyin and livin with this shit everywhere and all they do is act like it never happened, and they want to blame me? (*Beat*) No, I'm not going mad. I'm not crazy and I'm definitely not happy and I'm not gonna lose my mind in here. I am not forgettin who I am. (*She pulls away from Swagger. She takes a rapid beat, steps onto the chair and then onto Swagger's desk.*) My name is DELPHINIA and DELPHINIA is a constellation and constellations don't die. They live forever in the sky. Just look to the sky and you'll see DELPHINIA! (*With effort she regains her composure, sits on table, and then takes a cigarette from out of Swagger's pack.*) I need a match. (*Beat*) What do cigarettes do? Don't they kill people?

The Adventures of Munchkin Woman

JEAN KRISTEN HEDGECOCK

The WOMAN is in her late 20s, early 30s.

WOMAN: I'm walking down the block, right, and it's pouring—like end of the world rain. And those umbrellas that they sell as you walk out of the subway stations, the black ones, they're always black, they're three dollars for a reason. About three minutes from the place you buy them, they turn inside out, or fly away. I know. It's happened to me several times, and you'd think I'd learn my lesson, but noooo. Maybe a dollar a minute of dryness is worth it, I don't know, I haven't decided yet. But the point is my umbrella is more like a cape flapping behind me in the wind and it's freezing and I'm soaked and all I want to do is get in a taxi, but trying to get a taxi in New York in the rain is like a man trying to find . . . you know. Just when you think he's there . . . nope. It's better to just do it yourself, *get* there yourself, I mean, which is why I was walking, but suddenly the wind picks up a little and before I know it, I'm floating, like flying kind of. You all think I'm making this up, but I swear it's true. And I landed right across the street from a Dunkin' Donuts. I wonder if it's a mirage or if I'm dreaming, or if maybe there really is a god, one that cares about *me*. . . . I jump over the puddles in leaps and bounds, my umbrella cape flying behind me and I open the front door and fly inside, and right there standing in front of me, biting into a French cruller is the single most handsome man I've ever seen. He smiles at me, and I make a mad dash to the bathroom to fix myself up a bit, only there was no bathroom, just a telephone booth, so I ducked in there and, gosh . . . I'm embarrassed to say . . . oh, what the hell, I'll probably never see you people again, I took all my clothes off. Well, not all of them, of course, I left my undergarments on . . . and my umbrella cape. Why are you looking at me like that? You're judging me, I'll bet. You are, and you don't even know me. Alright look, let me tell you this . . . I was soaking wet, you want me to sit around in wet clothes? I would have gotten sick. . . . (*As if letting them in on a secret.*) And also, I have a fabulous body, and well, I thought it would be my best shot at attracting Cruller Man. So, I walk out there, and he's sipping his coffee, and I lean up against the counter and I'm waiting for him to say something. In the meantime, I ordered a hazelnut coffee and 16 Munchkins. I figured that by the time I finished all the Munchkins, we would have made our first date. But by the time there were only three left, he still hadn't said anything . . . so, I walked over to him and I said, "Hey Cruller Man, can I interest you in a Munchkin or two or three?" And do you know that man just put his coat on and walked out. Didn't even say a word to me. Maybe he didn't speak English. Of course! I don't know why that didn't occur to me sooner. Anyway, I still had my hazelnut coffee and three more Munchkins, and I decided to sit for a while, either until my clothes dried or until it stopped raining—the Dunkin' Donuts is open 24 hours. Do you want to know what happened next? In walks another amazingly handsome man, I'm not kidding, maybe even *more* handsome than Cruller Man. I looked at him and smiled, and he dashed past me, past the glass display of donuts, past the tables littered with coffee cups and right into . . . guess where? The phone booth! And he came out bare-chested and in boxers, and he looked me in the eye and said, "Hello, Munchkin Woman, I'm chocolate-frosted, sprinkled donut man." And I smiled and offered him my last remaining Munchkin, which I knew I had been saving for a reason, and don't you know he took it! He asked me if I wanted to go somewhere a little more cozy, and I said that I did, of course. And when he turned to leave, I saw that he was wearing a three-dollar umbrella cape, too, and I was suddenly very, very happy. And I stood on the corner in my underwear, while chocolate-frosted, sprinkled donut man walked to the edge of the curb in his boxers, and wouldn't you know the moment he put his hand up, a taxi pulled right over—on the very first try. It wasn't until the next morning that we realized we had left our clothes in the Dunkin' Donuts, but it didn't matter, it was still raining, and I was still wearing my cape, so I just jumped out the window and flew home.

Excerpt from *Mitzi's Abortion*

ELIZABETH HEFFRON

MITZI, 23, sits uncomfortably at a restaurant, opposite her soon-to-be ex-husband, Chuck. Throughout the following she avoids looking at him.

MITZI: And . . . at some point . . . before everything gets rolling, somebody gives you this little book. I can't remember who . . . maybe the social worker. But, it's this book about stillbirth, right? Called "When Hello Means Goodbye."

And inside, they give you all this like practical advice, about what to do when you know you're going to deliver a dead baby. They suggest that you should, like, name the baby. That you . . . look at him, you know? When he comes out. Which sounds so awful and gross, because based on his problems, you're imagining this horrible monster. So, at first, these things seem really sick to you. Or at least they did to me . . . They even tell you to hold him, and photograph him, and you think, oh my God, these people are nuts! You know? I mean how disgusting . . . (*Beat*) But . . . then he finally comes. And you can't help it . . . you're like drawn to his face, his quiet, bruised little body. And he doesn't look hideous at all, just . . . really, really tired. And there are even certain family features that you recognize. And he's got these perfect little feet and hands. And suddenly, you are just . . . so happy! About the sheer, like, REALness of these appendages. You know? They exist! They have been alive. And they opened and closed up into tiny little fists, and beat on you from the inside, as if saying, "Hurry up and check me out, I won't be around for long." And it just feels really good to know that you have not made this little guy up! That he was real. And . . . even though . . . I can already see he's fading from my family and friends, and stuff . . . I don't think he's ever gonna fade for me, you know? Because no one else ever felt him, knew him when he lived. Only me. Only me, you know Chuck . . . ?

(*Mitzi finally looks at Chuck and gauges his reaction.*)

Excerpt from *Distance Over Time Equals*

LINDSAY BRANDON HUNTER

MARIA gets home after losing the job that defines her.

MARIA: On the way home, I stopped at the store because I wanted a banana. My mother grew up on the Alaskan panhandle, when Alaska was still a territory, and bananas were a special treat. Something unusual. She got one in her Christmas stocking every year. I think they also ate cheese that came out of jars. Anyway. I tend to think of them—bananas, I mean—as generally available. When you want a banana, you can find one.

Except I couldn't. I asked the man in the produce department where they were and he said they were *out* of bananas. They didn't even have any brown spotty ones. So I went to another grocery store.

There were no bananas there, either. There was another produce man, so I asked him what was going on. Nothing is going *on*, he told me. We just don't have any. I was getting a little irritated. You always have bananas, I told him. Bananas are a fact of civilized life. I have never previously found you *bananaless*. I think something's going on.

He narrowed his eyes at me, and I thought he was going to get really mad, and I was about to say: Listen. It's been a real *day*, okay? And pretty much the only thing I can think of in this world that I want, that someone can *give* me, is a banana and I can't find one even though in this global economy they're about as tropical as athlete's foot cream—but I didn't, because it turned out he wasn't mad. He just started singing. And I couldn't believe that I hadn't seen it coming: *Yes, we have no bananas . . .* So I joined in: *We have no bananas today.*

I wonder what happens when they run out of carrots.

Anymore

CARLEEN JASPERS

GERMAINE, a woman in her 60s, is standing, looking out her beloved/haunted attic window. She is speaking to her daughter who is busy packing boxes behind her.

GERMAINE: Even when I was a little girl, I loved coming up here—probably because nobody else cared to. It was like having my own club house, only there weren't any other members—except for maybe the birds.

There used to be a hole right here through the roof where the stovepipe ran. In the winter, the birds were thick because of the heat. I used to sneak bread crusts up here after the dishes were done, and put them out on the roof and watch the birds peck. They were practically tame then.

One day, I remember spotting a dark, shiny bird—very different-looking from what we were used to. He was trying to get his share, only the other birds kept driving him away. I took pity on him and tossed a crust in his direction. He made a dive for it but got too close to the grate so he tumbled down inside the stovepipe. Got stuck below the big S-shaped curve. I could hear him in there fluttering around, chirping—completely helpless.

The stovepipe came apart in sections. I knew that because I'd watched Dad install it. I figured it was no big deal; we could take it apart and free him. When I mentioned this at supper, Dad seemed more than willing but Mother said, "Never! That bird is so filthy now from all that coal soot, he'll dirty up our whole house if you let him."

And so we didn't do anything. And every day when I came up here to put food out for the birds, I had to listen to his little wings beat and beat and beat against the stovepipe, and hear his chirps grow more 'n more dim until I . . . until I didn't think I could take it anymore.

Then one day, the noise stopped. And even though I didn't want to feel happy, I was. I was so happy because all I wanted was to have my place back, just like it used to be and not have to think about him anymore.

Excerpt from *Spring Thaw*

SUSAN JOHNSTON

BABS, 35, a stripper, talks to the audience.

BABS: Them. Grinding their erections into me. They could fuck me until I was raw and bleeding, I won't cum. Suck my clit for an hour, I won't cum. Women don't cum because we have to; we cum because we want to. It's like that. It's a choice to get off. So I choose to. When I was stupid and young, I used to believe it would work. Some fucker would be digging his way to China inside of me, tearing me to pieces, blood in the toilet in the morning and still, I'd lay there thinking, "Yeah, okay, this time, yeah, this is the one." And I'd arch my back and shimmy my ass like a good girl. Then I'd look in his eyes. And his eyes would be closed. Every time. Every guy. Finally, I fucking woke up and realized I could be faceless and nameless and still they'd cum. I could have been anyone. What the fuck did it matter? But back then, when I was an idiot, I would lay there, all hurt and shit, and stare at the ceiling, with them masturbating on top of me. And when I'd finally had enough of the banging and the ripping, I'd grind back. To get them off, to get them off, to get them off of me. And they'd explode like little boys playing with firecrackers. Their bodies heaped on my chest. I'd stroke their backs, silently wishing their limpness would fall out, their sweaty chests would follow their backs onto the sheets so I'd be released. But instead, he'd fall asleep, whoever he was, pinning my lungs into compressed gasps until I'd have to roll him over myself. And he wouldn't even notice. They never notice.

Cowslips

HONOUR KANE

Rural Ireland, 1943. The depression years. NOELEEN O'HONE *is a nomadic ingénue of 22.*

NOELEEN: My family. We had a dairy shop with a 115-cattle-strong yard in the arse of Dublin City. Our house was like a railway station. Thick with cockle men, cattle jobbers, dairy boys coming and going. Going and coming all hours the day, all days the year. All the years and all the years for seven generations. Calling down through time, "Great weather for the animals, thank the Holy God."

There's Sanctus Boffin, the oldest cow we ever owned. She's baldy. Ghostly pale with red hairs lining her wrinkles. Her milk is kept in the specials, cause Daddy says it's cream.

I love Patrick's Day and the cows going out to the fields for summer. Love calving time, when I carry newborned calves in from the meadows. I sit at the back of our motorcar, their weeshy heads laid in me lap. The one time, a calf was named for me, "Noeleen O'Honeen."

I member. Member that one morning's early when Daddy cried, "Christ of Compassion, the foot and mouth has hit the town. It's in the yard. It's in the yard. Cows and trousers—even the wind—will walk it into every farm in Ireland afore the week is out."

That day. That day, I mitched from school to see the cattle being shot in Phoenix Park. There were thousands and thousands of cows there. I caught sight of Daddy and follied him. He was searching for Sanctus Boffin, the oldest cow we ever owned. He took a gun from the soldiers and BANG, shot her down. She fell and she fell right into the pit.

The pit. Thick with dead cows piled high. And the burning, the pyres burning. The smoke. And roar of our empty fields. Our ever emptering hills the length, the very breath of Ireland.

As I breathed in that stinking hell, I knew. Knew I'd never slide down hay again. Never walk our cows to grass of a Patrick's Day. And never carry my wee calf home. My sweet Noeleen O'Honeen. Never bring her. Never bring her home of a March morning.

Shoes

AURORAE KHOO

SYLVIA, 50s, is an Asian immigrant to San Francisco. She is a hunchback. Strauss's "Emperor's Waltz" comes on. Sylvia waits, as if at a cotillion.

SYLVIA: My sister came to live with me in San Francisco. Arrived just to tell me I don't know about love, romance, anything. But I know. These answers can be found in dancing. You see, I do this dance, or I used to do this dance. 1, 2, 3 . . . 1, 2, 3 . . . 1, 2, 3 . . . 1, 2, 3. . . . (*Sylvia begins to waltz with an imaginary partner.*) It was a waltz, down the street, anywhere. I'd waltz behind mailboxes, trees, street lamps. Anything I could hide behind, so I could look at men's shoes. 8, 9, 10 are the sizes of my choice. 1, 2, 3 . . . 1, 2, 3 . . . 1, 2, 3 . . . Our father's black wingtips taught us how to waltz. Look down, follow the steps, and they spin you around. 1, 2, 3 . . . 1, 2, 3 . . . 1, 2, 3. . . .

It's my mating ritual. But I mate alone. I'm much too shy to mate with anyone else. When I dance, I can't bring myself to look into my partner's eyes. I just look down, away, at their shoes. Why, I've been bending over looking at shoes so long my back has curved into the letter 'C.' Among company, my sister has even called me . . . a hunchback! This is not very good for waltzing. But I don't care. I don't care what she says.

My back is the result of romance! I'll see a lovely pair of loafers, oxfords, or lug-heeled boots on the street. And from afar, I'll bend over and watch them. Watch the sole swivel. The laces expand and contract. The leather chafe against the heel. They may be waiting at a bus stop, jumping over dog shit, or ensnared in a piece of ill-disposed gum, but they move

64

as if there was music in them. And everything in me follows them, dances after them. Waltzes behind them into a restaurant, through a park. And I know, with all my heart, that the man in them is beautiful. Only beautiful men wear lovely shoes. I've always been afraid to look above the knees, so I must admit . . . nothing with these men has ever worked out.

But now, now it's different. Mark my word. I am in love. In love with a pair of waltzing white bucks. And he's going to fix my back. So I can look in his eyes. (*She begins to dance again, counting time.*) 1, 2, 3 . . . 1, 2, 3 . . . 1, 2, 3. . . . (*Giggling.*) My heart pounds hard when he comes to see me. Eyes are so much more frightening than shoes.

And What She Told Me

MARTY KINGSBURY

CYBELLE, a woman in her 30s, is alone on stage.

CYBELLE: She said he hit her. Repeatedly it happened and repeatedly she told me. Hit her with hand or with belt, with glove or with tie, hit her nude or hit her clothed, hit her singing or hit her silent, on the body, on the hand, on the head, on the meat, on the beat of the clock, tick, tick, tick, tick.

She said he said kneel and she knelt. She said he said sing and she sang. She said he said open and she opened. She said he said give and she gave. She said he said silence and her world was an echo of the past. She gave him her trust. He gave her her fear. And she said he would not hold, would not touch, would not care, except as a statue made of cold cold stone.

She said she had tried to tell, that they blocked their eyes and said have another cookie, have another valium, have a little more silence in your room alone, there there. You're going to the doctor, you're going for some tests, it's going to take some time alone, there, there. She said she told teachers and nursemaids, psychiatrists and doctors, interns and ward nurses, friends and cousins, but she got another cookie, she got another valium, she got more silence in her room alone, there, there.

Excerpt from *Original Sin*

LISA M. KONOPLISKY

BRIDGET, late 20s to early 30s, addresses her sexual abuse survivor's group.

BRIDGET: The last straw? I'd have to say Sam's Club. Yeah . . . um . . . What? No, it was definitely that last trip to Sam's. I'd promised myself, yeah, I'd promised. I said I'd never go again . . . at least not alone . . . but it was Sunday night and . . . I don't know how this happened cause I'm usually so careful about this kind of thing, but . . . but it was Sunday night and I needed . . . no, you don't understand, I really needed those latex gloves. . . . I could have just popped by the 24-hour Walgreens . . . but at Sam's, you know, they sell them in bulk. So I said, "O.K., I'm going" and before you know it I'm in the car and then the next minute there I am in the Sam's Club parking lot and that place never seems safe, I'm telling you, drivers are always going the wrong way, especially the seniors . . . the chances of them killing you are HUGE . . . ABSOLUTELY ENORMOUS . . . beyond that even. So finally I'm there but I'm not getting paper towels. I'm floating up and down the aisles like a spirit, like I'm powered by some force beyond my ken and I know that they're taking the oxygen out of the air. They can do that, you know. They do it so you can't decide, so you stay there for hours, so you can't know your own mind . . . that's why they do it . . . they know what it takes . . . to get people to buy these things . . . these big, these HUGE THINGS . . . and suddenly I feel . . . no . . . I know . . . that my heart is breaking. . . . I'm looking at the meats aisle and I'm thinking of those eyes . . . cow eyes asking, why are you here? . . . where are the paper towels? . . . and I feel the pain . . . it's falling out of everything, cascading from those high shelves into the enormous containers of Miracle Whip and JIF . . . always the smooth and never, never, NEVER the chunky and it's like . . . it's like they're too stingy . . . like the world is too stingy for the chunks . . . we're all too fucking stingy for the chunks . . . those little bits of things insisting, "This is what we were, this is what we were once, we were peanuts, we had likes and dislikes, we had families, we had beauty contests where we decided who was the most beautiful peanut, the most poised, the most congenial. Do you know what it's like to watch your whole family ground into PASTE . . . not incinerated, not released into a nothingness, a death, but reduced, less than what they were—but still the essential nut—and given, packaged and sealed for someone else's pleasure. A paste."

And I felt the pain and horror of all those nuts and all that paste and other things . . . vanilla beans and Styrofoam plates and tampons . . . they come from cotton, I think . . . the sheep hunted and clubbed to death. Who stands up for them? Do you know what I'm talking about, when you can feel the pain, hear your heart breaking, feel it crack down the middle like . . . what are they? Sutures, fissures . . . the things on your skull . . . and just then over the P.A.—that song from the 80s . . . do you remember? . . . Taco, that weird fella named Taco . . . singing "Puttin' On The Ritz." (*Singing, or sing-talking.*) "If you don't know where to go TO why don't you GO where fashion SITS. Puttin' on the RITZ." That weird rhythm of the words and then I heard it in their voices and I knew that the pain was everywhere, seeping out of every pore of Sam's Club, like an enormous body, breathing and hurting, wounded black and blue with tears and a crown of those thorns and blood running down.

I had to stop, actually stop and sit down, I sat down on a carton of jam . . . Smucker's . . . I think . . . and I had to wonder, honestly, are latex gloves this difficult for other people or is it just me?

Diet Cherry Coke

SHERRY KRAMER

The end of the world is perhaps a month or two away. Sex is just about the only comfort or joy left to people, but LISA has lost faith in it.

LISA: Here's the thing that's got me stumped. If sex is so great, why hasn't it made this country greater? I mean think of all the sex we've had. We've been having and having and having it, we have more sexual access to each other than any other civilized—and I use the term loosely—nation on earth. Our children are now sexually active almost from birth. Does it make us more compassionate? No. Does it make us, as a people, more—interesting? Self-reflective? Better girl scouts, better politicians, better at chess, gardening, structural engineering, or, and this is the sore spot as far as I am concerned—better at sex? No. Sex, the sex everybody is having, in real life now, in celluloid now, and in data bit stream now—none of it even makes us better at sex. Which should be the least of its consequences, don't you think, huh? Even if it doesn't give us a more robust relationship with our community, our nation, our god.

I just don't get it. Why didn't it change the air, the atmosphere, the kindness available. Why didn't it make us all better people who could change the world. Why didn't it at least make better television. Those writers, those story editors, they had a lot of sex, god, I knew the story editor of that show, what was it called, you know the one, the one on Monday nights we used to watch, yeah, that one, well that guy had the biggest dick I ever saw, and that show was not that good. I mean, proportionally, you know.

So when someone asks me to have sex now—I ask them. I ask them, What's so great about sex? And you know what? They don't know. What they know is nothing. Because sex is not great. If it were great, it would have transformed the world while there was still time. Like Martin Luther King. Or Ghandi. Sex is not great. It's just bigger than you are. The thing about sex is, it's like a diet cherry coke—you drink one of them, you drink a million of them, there's no effect, because there's no nutrition, no lasting, lingering, fundamental point to it. Not after one diet cherry coke, not after a million. No nutrition. Sure, there's 12 ounces of pleasure, there's excitement—the bump from the caffeine, the lie of the counterfeit sweetness, the whisper that this is happiness. But one diet cherry coke—a million diet cherry cokes. No difference. And that's what sex is. Nothing, after it's over, that's different, that doesn't go down the drain.

It's as special as two people get, but it doesn't make them special.

FantasyLand

MARY LATHROP

DAPHNE, 40 or older, does some late-night channel surfing while her husband snores beside her.

DAPHNE: So okay, it's late at night. Lochinvar has fallen asleep over one of those engineering magazines he's always bringing to bed with him, his reading light on, stupid little half-glass bifocals sliding down his nose, his mouth slack and open. I mean, when you're married to them, they're not always that attractive, quite the contrary, so instead you're going to think about a sexy man. Think about his sexy mouth, imagining his chest has just a little bit of hair, tight and curly, you know, just around the nipples. . . . And you throw back your head, and your hair falls off your shoulders, just tickles the backs of your own shoulders, and the corners of his lips, just the corners are smiling at you, and you feel yourself fall into his eyes, and everything is starting, and then he runs his finger down your neck, just like that, and you see his mouth say "I want you."

Only then Romeo here starts doing that awful snuff, snuff snoring, and you have to tell him, "Bill, roll over, roll over, honey," only Bill's not rolling tonight. So you give up and turn on *Nightline* where Ted Koppel is interviewing some boring body about some boring billion dollar debt for . . . You know, Ted Koppel has a kind of interesting laugh, no, it's not really a laugh, it's more of a, of a chuckle, actually.

And so I am . . . not in my bed with my husband. No . . . I'm in . . . a hotel suite. Yes. And I am here because . . . in the morning I'm making America's presentation to the U.N. about the billion dollar debt! And Ted Koppel is on his way over here right this second to brief me. I go to my suitcase,

just to unpack, and pull out—surprise!—an important neg-
ligee. Wait a second, wait, how did nine hundred dollars
worth of handmade French silk get inside my bag? A surprise
from Bill? Bill doesn't believe in surprises, and anyway, he's
not going to spend the nine hundred when the house needs a
new roof next year. A little love note—Bill never writes notes:
"To my only wife, my dearest wife: It's making me sick to my
stomach that we're apart, but don't think about me. I am so
proud of your important work for our country. If only I could
be there to slip off this nightie tonight. Tomorrow, knock 'em
dead at the United Nations. Yours faithfully, Bill."

Start again. Bill is fine, he's on the other side of the conti-
nent, I don't have to think about him, whereas I am in a hotel
room in a glamorous far-away city, and I'm here because . . .
just because. And I'm wearing . . . my sweats. A knock at the
door—it's Ted Koppel, who it turns out, has a rather sexy
chuckle, and he's here because—come on, come on, keep it
simple—because he sat next to me on the airplane and we,
well, we just caught fire with each other. Huh, Ted Koppel sat
next to me on the airplane. Ted Koppel would definitely sit in
first class. I flew first class? How did I come up with a first
class airplane ticket? My darling Bill insisted that I use up all
his frequent flyer miles so that my flight might be enjoyable.
Don't I even have a heart? I used up all of Bill's hard-earned
miles on a transcontinental flirtation with Ted Koppel!

I'm staring into the face of Ted Koppel. I don't know anything else. Ted, he says to me with that sexy chuckle, you
know he has that sexy chuckle, he says, "We have some
unfinished business." "How did you find me, Ted?" No, forget
that part, it's too complicated: taxi cabs, explanations . . . And
you've got to set the scene, go shopping for new underwear,
figure a way out of your clothing, choose a caterer.

I'm sitting on the deck of a million dollar yacht somewhere in the Aegean. I'm drinking a champagne cocktail and
sunning myself naked, no, uh—no, I'm wearing a long, gauzy
caftan. Ted Koppel, whose chuckle is sexier than ever, no

longer appears on *Nightline*. No, now he's a fabulously wealthy French shipping magnate. Yes. And he's younger now, too, maybe only forty. Actually, he isn't Ted Koppel at all. No, he's, he's . . . He's Andy Garcia! YES!!!

He wants me. Andy Garcia is hungry for ME. The hot sun is beating in the rhythm of my heart. Andy Garcia says, he says to me, Andy says, "Darling," oh! and my caftan magically dances away in the warm Aegean breeze. And Garcia, he drinks in my body with his bedroom eyes, his sexy eyes, and he says, he says to me, Andy Garcia says, "What are these lines on your stomach? Uucccch, what is this—cottage cheese on your thighs?" And he leaps overboard and swims away . . . Bye, Andy. Why is it so hard to get this right?

Unlike with Bill. With Bill, it's actually an amazingly simple task to get it just right. I mean, he's the one who put ice on my neck when I puked for months with morning sickness, both times, with both babies. Who always sends roses the day before our anniversary, so that when he sees them he'll actually remember that it's our anniversary, and in case he does forget, well then, he's already sent the roses, hasn't he? That is so sweet. Who still kisses this sagging, lumpy body, and tells me with a straight face and in all sincerity that I'm beautiful—not beautiful to him—beautiful. Who says, and I quote, that he wants to fuck me when I'm ninety. Ninety.

Bill.

So you carefully slide his stupid glasses off of his nose, put them on the nightstand, take the engineering magazine out of his sleeping hands, mark the page so he can read it some more tomorrow night, lean across him, turn off the lamp, tap him softly on the shoulder, tell him, "Bill, roll over; roll over, honey," and when he rolls, you spoon up against him in the dark, run your fingers through the hair on his chest, just a little, you know, just the way he likes, just around the nipple, and you whisper in his ear, "I want you. I want you."

Excerpt from *String of Pearls*

MICHELE LOWE

KYLE talks to the audience.

KYLE: I bathe her, I dress her, I carry her up and down two flights of stairs. I shave her legs, brush her teeth, change her diaper. She recognizes my sister when she comes to see her. She can tell you what she had for dinner last night, but for some strange reason, she has no idea who I am. My mother thinks I'm her nurse. Every Friday afternoon she tries to pay me.

I work nights at the funeral home. I get a nap in the afternoon while Mom watches TV, then we go for an iced coffee at Dunkin' Donuts. She remembers that she likes Dunkin' Donuts.

When I break out in hives on my back and shoulders, Dr. Beckman says it's a reaction to my fatigue. He tells me to check Mom into that nursing home in New City, just for the weekend so I can get some rest. Is he kidding? We don't have money for that. He gives me ointment for my itch and I go home.

But the ointment doesn't work and the hives spread to my face and my neck. People are starting to stare at me. I'm getting less sleep now because Mom's skipping her afternoon nap. And I'm changing her twice before dinner because she keeps shitting herself—

My brother loses one of his jobs so he cuts back on what he sends us. I'm living on one turkey sandwich a day, and we're getting behind on the gas and electric but I make sure she gets clean clothes and her pink donut and a bath on the second floor because she doesn't like the goddamn tub on the first floor and she's still calling me Miss and this is four years

I'm doing this, four years. And every night I pray that when I wake up she'll be good and dead—
SO I CAN GET OUT THE FUCK OUT OF HERE.

Excerpt from *Iphigenia and Other Daughters*

ELLEN MCLAUGHLIN

IPHIGENIA is the daughter of Agamemnon, general of the Greek army. The army and its fleet are stalled at Aulis, waiting for a wind that will allow them to set sail for Troy to begin the Trojan War. Due to an affront committed by the army against Artemis, the winds have been stopped. The Goddess demands a human sacrifice or she won't let the winds blow. Agamemnon is persuaded that he must bring his eldest daughter, Iphigenia, to Aulis on the pretext that she will marry the great warrior Achilles. Then he must sacrifice her himself or the winds will never blow favorably and the fleet will be stalled indefinitely. He eventually goes along with the ruse and summons his daughter to Aulis.

IPHIGENIA:
In a windless place everything is eternal and bland
Nothing can be changed here
It all hums in terrible clarity
With no wind to transform, modify or shift anything
Feathers fall from a plucked chicken
And make a neat circle that stays and stays
There is a leaden singularity to each thing
Each color immobile
Everything has become too important here
Like something stared at too long
Until it might as well be anything
A person could go mad
As my mother combed my hair this morning
Each broken strand

Slunk down and coiled where it fell
Separate and smug as etched spirals on the floor
Bride
What is it to be a bride here?
In this windless place
A bleached column?
A sliver of standing bone?
But perhaps that will not happen
Nothing can happen here I think
It is a place of dead air.

Nothing more useless than ships
Miles—could it be miles—of them?
Lined up
Hauled up
Tilting
Impossible
Baking in the sun
Nosing the water which barely moves
As if the ocean were some bloated pond
That was what I saw first
So many useless ships
Bristling for such a distance along a flaccid shore
That was before my occupation became clear
My occupation as *something which is visible*
Because then we descended to walk among the men
Cities full
All of them watching me
What do they see, I wonder?
I am like Medusa, I change men to silent stone
Games stop, stories break at their start
And nothing stirs as I pass
Only their eyes, turning in their sockets
Such silence, such level dust
I am some phantom
No one in this dress

I am not here
I am just some spell that is cast
It is a powerless power
Like this wind which is only remarkable in its absence

Helmets, lances, gold and iron skins they have
And me in this thin dress
It's a predicament.

They killed a deer yesterday
I saw it while it was still running
Stamping down the boughs
Cracking its forest
Spotting through the stricken trees
Suddenly so visible
All of them running after it, not losing sight
There I go, I thought, run fast
But they caught it
Of course
And when they brought it in
Limp and undignified, head lolling
I couldn't watch, I turned away
Because the eyes were open
And they saw me
Dead, they saw me
I shivered
You and me, I thought
We know each other
They offered me the heart
Nice of them, I guess
But I said something
And backed away
They watched me, of course
All the way to the tent
So many eyes glittering in the fire light
Fixed on me diminishing

Until the flap swallowed me and I became invisible again
And they could turn and eat
I hold the darkness to my face
As if it were food

But something is wrong
My parents thrash at each other in the woods
Out of ear shot
But there is screaming
Mother comes back, eyes swollen, face streaked
And smashes my head to her breast
Squeezing my ribs
I can't breathe I am so dear to her
Father stood in the tent for awhile yesterday
He looks ill and won't meet my eyes
He won't touch me
Who is this husband?
What is this marriage?
Tonight the ritual knives are being sharpened on stone
Tonight there are figures circling the fire, all in black,
Telling hymns I don't know
What kind of marriage are we preparing?
I thought I would wear flowers
But nothing grows here
I thought there would be women
There are no women
Are there no other girls in the world?
Suddenly I am the last and only girl
And all these turning faces, all these anxious idle fingers
All these men to satisfy
This is the bride
The only bride

Morning comes and I am a white dress
Walking up the crumbling cliff as if I know where I am going
What I'm doing

To meet him
Whoever he might be
I am ascending to the altar
I look down from a great height to see how the ships still lie
Splayed like broken teeth
Today the light is merciless
And sound would travel if there was sound
But there is only my feet on the pebbles
That hurl themselves down to the ships as I pass
I come to the altar
But there is no one
Just the black–shrouded priests
And there my father
Who has made his face a stranger
Eyes locked in their sockets
Dull as coal
And a knife
But where are the animals?
Poor innocents
With the last cropped grass still in their moist mouths
But there is only me
And all the eyes are on me
Visible me
This is a terrible place
Something must be done
Ah. I see.
I was right
Here is my husband
This ancient stone
And the quick shadow of the knife
I am to marry everyone
Every single one
This is what it is at last.

A Tradition

ANA MARIA MEBANE

JULIA, a woman in her early 30s, stands at her kitchen counter with all the ingredients for making cornbread in front of her. As she mixes the ingredients, she speaks to her daughter.

JULIA: My mother used to make me cornbread from scratch. I used to say when I grow up, I'm gonna make this bread here for my daughter, and she'll make it for her daughter and it will become what they call a tradition. Now I don't know precisely what scratch means, but I'm gonna try my darnedest to make some tonight and then turn that scratch into cornbread. I knew Mommy loved me when she'd make me her cornbread. Said it was special. Special for me. So tonight this cornbread I'm making is special for you. Granted, I'm not much of a cook. But any idiot can cook. It's just chemistry. Well, maybe that's not the best comparison, since chemistry is hard, but it's like . . . It's like putting things together. Like getting dressed. (*She starts to cry.*)

Sweetie, Sweetie, Mommy's not hurt. No, no, Sweetheart, I'm fine. Don't you worry. I have low self-esteem. There's nothing to be ashamed of. You'll probably have low self-esteem, too, one day, and that's okay. Before Oprah, I was fat and useless, but now I have low self-esteem. . . . When I stop and think of everything that woman has done for American families . . . Ever since your daddy left, I've been trying to, uh, reframe things, you know? Like outside today, it's not awful; it's just gray. Well, maybe not gray—silver! So I wake up, I look outside, and I think to myself: It's silver out. And then, you see, it's not so bad. You've got to see the positive! Or else what is the point? Because at some point you're gonna wonder what the point is and unless you see the positive in every little thing you're not going to know the point, and there is a point, and that's . . . positivity! So that's what we'll do today; we'll reframe things. We didn't wake up late this morning; we slept in, right?

And when I think about your daddy, it's not that we got a divorce, it's that we amicably split. You know? Just sort of . . . (*She does a splitting gesture.*) No one's mad. No reason to be mad. Amicable. (*Pause*) See, also, it's not that your daddy was a faggot, that's a bad word, Honey; we don't say that word; it's that he was a homosexual. You know what that means, Honey? It means he never loved Mommy, okay, Sugar-bear?

Oh, I bet he loves you. I sure do. I bet he does. (*Pause*) You know what, Sweet-pea? Mommy's not going to make you any cornbread. Mommy doesn't want you to get chubby, and Oprah said something about bread and carbs. Why don't you be a good little girl, and go for a jog?

A Bear Incident

SUSAN MENDELSOHN

A WOMAN, about 50 years of age, is standing in a spotlight in the middle of a stage with a backpack on her back. She is dressed for hiking.

WOMAN: Never run. No. Never run from a grizzly bear. It triggers something in them. This is a situation where fight or flight will not serve you. Fight and you're bound to lose. Run and you're bound to lose. Did you know that a grizzly can run at speeds of 35–40 miles an hour? Never run. Never run from a grizzly.

Those moments in the wilderness, like meeting a grizzly, those moments when you wish you could run but cannot. Those are called encounters. That's what the National Park Service calls them. Encounters. Not be confused with an incident.

An incident—one of those unpleasant moments that you shove out of your memory like it never happened. You know (*wags her finger*), "I never had sex with that woman." That Thomas guy on the Supreme Court. Just shove that unpleasant moment into some drawer in your psyche that you'll never open. Those are incidents.

But encounters . . . You are supposed to report bear encounters. It's supposed to help the next hiker who comes along. I'm not sure it's good for the bear. Encounters. That's when you're in a situation that is dangerous. Not imagined dangerous, but really dangerous. Like 500-plus pounds or more is going to kill you and eat you. Now, that's an encounter.

One of those moments when you meet one of the few living things that's higher on the food chain than you. Even a gun wouldn't help you unless you were either a true marksman or just damn lucky. Lord knows, I'm not a marksman. And time keeps proving to me that I am not one of the lucky ones. A marksman would have to be able to find a bear's heart and send the bullet right to it. Have you ever noticed how those guys that just send a bullet to your heart don't have one? They must have read about the heart in a book somewhere or seen a diagram of where it's supposed to be. Even if I had a gun, I couldn't be a true marksman. I have enough of a heart to not have the heart to go for the heart. If you know what I mean. I don't have that killer instinct. Like the grizzly bear. The killer instinct. That thing that you trigger if you start to run.

And don't scream either. That sets the grizzly off, too. Not a lot of options you might say. Don't run. Don't scream. Not so. If you have the time, you can run up a tree. But . . . grizzlies can climb trees. So I guess you should forget about the tree.

(*She spies a berry bush and picks some to eat.*) Bears love berries. Oooh . . . these are really good. You're probably wondering what I'm doing here. (*Eats another berry.*) Hmmm . . . I hope they're not staining my teeth—talking to myself like I'm one goddamned monologue. Well, I'll tell you. (*Eats another berry.*) You don't want to surprise a bear. Some people wear those little bells and go around the trails sounding like cattle. But if you're in conversation, the sound of your voice will alert the bear. Do you see someone with me? Of course not, he's a quarter mile behind me. And even if he was with me, we wouldn't be in conversation. But that's another story—an incident, if you will. He'll catch up. Eventually.

So, you're in bear country and you surprise a bear. Uh-oh. What to do? First off—DO NOT look a bear in the eyes. That is taken as a sign of aggression. And then those ears will set back and get ready for a charge. No. Talk softly with your head off to the side. Like so. (*She puts her head to the side in a deferential position.*) If you'd like, you can extend your arms off to the side to give the bear the impression that you're bigger than you really are. (*She assumes this position, almost like Christ hanging from the cross.*)

This position was like the one my husband took when he told me he was leaving me. Couldn't look me in the face. His syllables had no inflection. After twenty-five years, there was no discussion on the matter. It was a simple statement. "I'm leaving. I'm not happy. I didn't know that this was what marriage was like. Good-bye." Where are you going? I asked him. He rattled a new apartment key in front of my face. It sounded like the bear bells I gave him for this hike. (*She chimes her bear bells.*) I begged him to stay a few more weeks. Until Christmas was over and the kids returned to college. But no. When you gotta go, you gotta go, I guess.

Speak with a low voice and back away. The bear doesn't want an encounter anymore than you do.

Let's say the bear is not bluffing. He's going to charge. That deferential position is not going to work. The bear sees through you. You really aren't bigger than you really are. All is not lost.

You can throw your backpack away as a diversion. (*She takes her backpack off and swings it away but does not let go.*) Or . . . (*she catches the pack*) you keep the backpack on . . . (*she puts the backpack back on*) . . . and drop. (*She does.*) Face down. Like this. (*She has her hands covering the back of her head as she drops to her knees and bends over, almost fetal-like.*) You can grab your legs tight into you. You know how when it hurts? Hurts so bad. Like someone has punched you in the stomach. Like someone has knocked the wind out of you? And all they used was words? "You're not fun anymore. You went and got old." You just want to curl up and die. There is this instinct, this instinct to protect yourself, to protect what's left of yourself, to protect something vital. It's the guts . . . (*She rises.*) Look here—what's the part you always read about when they've found a human carcass, something the bear ate but didn't finish. It's the guts that are missing. They go straight for the guts. They don't eat the head. Oh, they might crunch down on it. That is if they're merciful. But it's the guts they eat. (*Almost hissing.*) They eviscerate you. (*She swats at a mosquito on her arm.*) That's the problem with these early morning hikes. You get more wildlife. Of all sorts. (*She sees blood on her arm.*) Drat. That thing got me. (*She sucks her arm, rubs it.*)

Viagra, schmiagra . . . He might be able to get it up, but he sure is having a hard time keeping up. I can't believe . . . Yeah, right . . . You want me to sign some divorce papers? Take a hike with me, I tell him. Our son always tells me how you like to go hiking with Boopsie. Fresh meat. Isn't that what you told our son? Blonde, boobs, fresh meat you called it. Calling a woman fresh meat to my son. Fresh meat. Fresh meat doesn't smell. To us.

Smell is a bear's keenest sense. (*She pulls out a steak sealed in a ziplock bag from her backpack and swings it in front of her. She unzips it and the odor is obviously repugnant.*) Whew! Now, this is dead meat. If you were camping, you would know not to have *any* food odors around your tent. But, when hiking, it's best to just keep food well wrapped until you're ready to eat it. (*She waves the meat around some more.*) When hiking, there are two things you should always stay away from. A bear's carcass and bear's cubs. A grizzly will kill you defending either one of them. How to know a carcass? If you don't stumble across it, you will know it because of its stench. Something like this. (*Wrinkles up her nose in disgust and throws the meat in the direction of her as yet unseen husband.*) Mess with a bear's dead meat and *you're* dead meat.

Now, cubs may be cute. But if you come between a mother bear and her children, prepare to die. They will fight to the death to protect them. Even if the threat is imagined. And you know who these mothers have to defend their children against the most? The male grizzly. The male grizzly has no qualms against eating cubs. Especially after a long winter's nap. Even if they're his own. Not that he would *know* they were his own. He's long gone by the time they're born. But that mama bear will go up against a male twice her size protecting that cub. It's incredible.

But you know what else is incredible? After two or three years, mama bear's hormones start kicking in again. She gets horny. And she ditches those cubs. They try to come close to her. She swats at them. They don't understand. They don't understand things have changed. They try to come close to her again. She snarls at them. Maybe mama's playing, they think. They come close to nuzzle. She woofs at them. Woofs are *not* good. They're so confused. Mama walks away. "Of course, she's coming back." They wait. And they wait. But she doesn't come back. Not ever. Ever. Mother and child. Father and child. Husband and wife. They could cross each other's paths years later and they wouldn't even recognize each other. Isn't that incredible? How you could die protecting your own and then one day just switch it off and walk away? (*She freezes.*) Oh, my God! (*She turns in the direction of her as yet unseen husband. Whispering.*) It's a grizzly, an honest to god grizzly. (*Bear bells are heard in the direction of the unseen husband.*) It doesn't see me. (*She wets her finger and sticks it in the air.*) That's good. I'm upwind. That's good. But Harold . . . (*We hear bear bells. They're louder.*) Oh, dear. (*Bells are even louder.*) RUN, HAROLD!! RUN!! RUN FOR THAT TREE!!!! (*Offstage sound of frantic bear bell ringing.*) Maybe you'll be lucky. . . . (*We hear a man's heinous scream that lasts for five seconds and then abruptly stops.*)

If this were an encounter, I would notify the authorities. But this seems more like an incident to me. I'm not in danger anymore. Never scream. Never run. (*She slowly backs away upstage out of the light.*) Just speak quietly and slowly back away. (*Fadeout*)

Cockapoo

S.P. MISKOWSKI

GLORIA is a woman seeking employment.

GLORIA: I'm in training to be a Pest Control Protégé. That's what they call the cockroach-murdering sidekicks. Obviously, the company's not going to let us trainees loose on the public. We're only there to assist the real exterminators. Okay. I figure: "These people are professionals. There's nothing to worry about."

I meet my partner, my leader, my own, personal Exterminator. His name is Ed. He's fifty-four years old, he says, so don't fuck with him! I say: "Sure, Ed. No problem." Ed knows cockroaches like nobody's business, and he enjoys killing the suckers, it's almost a personal matter for the guy. My job, basically, is to wear this huge metal tank strapped to my back, and hold the hose up so Ed can find it when he needs it in a hurry. I'm not kidding. That's most of the job, right there. I get $12 an hour, so I strap on the tank.

I don't know if you've ever been stuck in traffic on a floating bridge inside a giant cockroach. Maybe you have. The worst part of driving a cockroach isn't that people stare. What bothers me is wondering if anyone I know is going to see me. I mean, if strangers saw me and didn't know it was me that would be okay. But I don't want to run into people I know and have them say: "Hey! Saw you riding around in a cockroach. What the hell?" Saying I make $12 an hour doesn't really explain it to somebody who doesn't need the money as bad as I do.

Finally, Ed pulls into a driveway. The house is a big, fat-assed, Tudor thing with a fancy door and a brass knocker.

This woman comes running out of the house, and she's wearing an actual maid's uniform and she's talking fast in Swedish or Norwegian. She waves her hands around in front of Ed, and points at the house. So I drag the gas tank out and we go into the house with this woman.

Now Ed is calling the maid "Annie" like they're best friends. In fact, he keeps touching her apron and touching her arm. I just tuned it out because I wanted the $12 an hour, and I did not want to fuck around with Ed and get fired. If this was a special favor or something, fine. Whatever. Who am I to question the wisdom of Ed?

Anyway, "Annie" kept walking on her tiptoes, kind of creeping along, and she made us do the same thing. We followed her to the basement. There was some really nice, expensive furniture down there, but most of it was broken. In the middle of the basement was a red velvet loveseat. One leg was busted, and it was kind of crushed down on the floor. "Annie" started talking fast in German or Swedish when she got to the loveseat, and she kept mumbling something to Ed about a "prabb-lemm . . . vermins . . . prabb-lemm. . . ."

In another room somewhere a dog was barking—a little dog, the kind that yaps when you leave it alone for too long. All of a sudden "Annie" got sick of the yapping and she opened a door and this dog, this miniature Cockapoo about the size of a donut, came hopping into the room. I heard it coming and I had my tank set on "safety" just in case. I wanted Ed to know he could count on me. At $12 an hour, I thought, he better be able to count on me, right?

What I didn't count on were the cockroaches.

Okay, look, they showed us *pictures* in training school. And we looked at some dead cockroaches. And we studied their life cycle and stuff. (Do you know how long a cockroach can live without its head attached to its body? You don't want to know.) So, I had the training and I thought I was ready for combat. But this was the real thing. Ed lifted a cushion on the loveseat and kind of—dropped it back in place. Then I heard a sound that made the hair stand up on my arms. I still hear it, sometimes, when I wake up in the middle of the night. Tiny legs and tiny feet and thousands of fuzzy little feelers. . . . From under the loveseat, all of a sudden came a big *wave* of cockroaches like a *mudslide*, pouring out in all directions! Sliding over everything: the tank, the loveseat, our feet, our legs . . .

I screamed and fell backward, over the dog. The maid screamed and tripped over Ed, who was trying to grab the dog away from the cockroaches that were just *swarming* over us. Ed screamed at me to get up and stop screaming, and the dog barked at the cockroaches, and "Annie" screamed at the dog, and I realized the "safety" wasn't on any more and my tank was making a hissing noise. . . .

Look, all I wanted was to make $12 an hour. And I wanted to get through my first day without any accidents. I did not sign on for the job out of a "mean streak" in my nature. I do not "hate animals." I did not go all the way to Bellevue to kill a customer's Cockapoo. It was never supposed to happen!

So: Yes, I do have pest control experience. But I'm looking to get into another line of work as soon as possible.

Neutered by Sperm

STEPHANIE MOORE

TRACY, thirty days sober, talks to her new sponsor.

TRACY: Don't know why you weren't invited. I think you were. Sure you were. Maybe. Maybe I was supposed to tell you. Maybe for sure. Hey, no worries. The party totally sucked, okay? It's all about this guy, Peter, who leaves his fat wife and goes to India and he just got back and it's his sobriety birthday, he's got fifteen years clear. Liar. You know me, right? *Let me be the first to slap your face.* But not today, today I want to support him. Truly. Even before I get there, I have like this fatal sense you know? Ever experienced that? The one that says you and this guy, this stranger, are important. To each other. This is the voice you ignore, right? But not tonight. Tonight I am an open book emotionally. Waiting for This Guy. Tonight's Prize Stranger. Tell him, you know, congratulations, this is the ME you've spent your entire repressed life waiting for. Not, hey, get an insight idiot. This is totally nondrinking. Sober as hell. Can you picture it? Really?

Anyway, the party. It was one of those well-heeled alcoholic's homes, the bleeding trail had more upkeep than the Golden Gate Bridge, you know the type? Ex-coke-dealer-sips-pear-juice, wearing the cool ripped jeans, pressed by illegal immigrants. The b-day guy, my future, call him Peter—they're all Peters, the ones who hook you—is standing by the door. Got the Aussie eyes and the Aussie hair and the Aussie vibes. Holds the door open like, I don't know, like, I'm returning from a shipwreck alive. *Well, well, well.* Actually stares deep into me. Those guys read your mind. Swear to God. They pull up your chart and spout it back to you. What?

Everything your last weenie boyfriend refused to say. Naturally, I emerge from the new womb, ready to spoon-feed him when the colon goes missing, ready to carry that nasty bag in my purse, all on account of a look. How sober is that? You see the guy and he sees you, no not like that, he *sees* you. Boom. Shit-hitting-fan. Kiss off ten years. So, you cut the deal with the eyes. Then to yourself, you say, is my alarm system, like, screaming here or is that my car? Slow way down. Back way the fuck off. Sociopaths buddy? My specialty. But he's not looking at me, why should he? The Blonde Nation, it's like they got their highlights together on the phone, before the party, and agreed to leather.

In my head, the new me is asking: is it fair, realistically, to get jealous before we've talked? You know? Kill the expectations, little assholes. And the I-just-want-to-slap-him, that feeling? Some kind of negative sign? Then he steps back, doesn't he? You've seen that, he always takes a steep step back. *Whoa babe. Met my match, ha!* I love that moment. Don't you love that moment? But then the new me realizes, he has to miss me. That sharp pang in the rib cage.

I keep right on walking.

I park myself by the sparkling water and nod at Texas Barbie 50th Anniversary with a headband. I pray for that woman, you know. Dear God, when I am her age, please, give me anything, give me a creaky walker, give me a failed hysterectomy, give me a screaming libido, but hold the headband. Fixated, I slam into the sliding glass door. God Speaks. Blammo. Instantly I regret my skintight pants. I regret my moldo shirt. I regret my see-through bra, what? Polyester Braille Babe. Why-oh-why did I wear that? Why do I always wear that?

See me. How raw is that?

So. Talk down to Nice Nobody by the sink, in order to keep an eye on you-know-who-is-holding-court. And I start to think, you know, I see myself in every blonde in the room. Suckered by sperm, I say this to my new self, not a life sentence, sweetheart.

I turn around. Jesus, he's alone now. What an acknowledgement. You know? It must be my turn. With my body, I tell him, I know you. Okay? Like I KNOW you. His body answers, yeah, he knows me too. Well, that could be promising. Or not. So we do nod-laugh. You know, deep. Deal with it, buddy. All those other notches on your belt, all those other GIRLS? Window-dressing. Say that with my look. Like, whammo, right? Life-changing experience, every hour on the hour. You read me? And I say, I've adopted someone in Nigeria and he says, adopt me, and I say, I will. I will take your bullshit self-construction and your walls and I will drive you to your knees. I figure I saved us both a few years.

Still Life of a Mouth

JULIE MARIE MYATT

A busy coffee shop. Day. The buzz of people laughing and talking, drowned out music of a woman singing. SOPHIE sits across from a man, whose back is to the audience.

SOPHIE: If I could tell you that a million times, I would . . . actually, I think I have and—but it hasn't changed a thing, has it? . . . my words have been repeated over and over in the air and still here I sit before you and you sit there unmoved by my lips moving and my declarations of love and someday, just someday I really think I might stop talking and walk away from the words I've said to you and find another vocabulary for a new man that isn't scared by my mouth and I might not need to say so very much to him right off the bat . . . we might just never need to say a thing and I could be the writer who coolly licks my lips and lays down my pen . . . and climbs into bed . . . and kisses the silence on your lips . . . I mean, his lips . . . see I've been counting my teeth lately and I find that behind each one, sits the traces of a thousand, a million, sentences . . . all the words that have ever come out of me and I can't help but wonder who is keeping track of all the things ever said to any person, all the people across the land . . . there's just no measure of all the words ever uttered and I somehow want some way to hold those things I've said, not just to you but to everyone I've ever encountered so that I might find the sum of my parts when the parts seem oddly unhinged . . . by silence . . . disjointed . . . maybe the words are the glue from which I am made . . . and yet I am stuck in this saying things . . . this constant saying things . . . explaining myself, expressing myself, explaining myself, aren't I? . . .

you don't have to answer that because you've already told me that I talk too much and while I don't disagree, I do maintain that you like me best when I'm talking . . . just not when I'm saying the things that you don't want to hear . . . right? . . . I don't know how to hold my tongue . . . not for long . . . but I have learned to stuff some things behind a tooth or two and now I think I have three new cavities . . . I do . . . something's rotting back there . . . I can feel it . . . that weird ache . . . down to the nerve . . . I think they're the few things I haven't said to you . . . like . . . "I'm scared" . . . "I'm leaving you forever" . . . "I'm sorry my mouth couldn't hold ours" . . . see, here I am getting all sentimental and you just wanted to say a quick hello . . . and this whole time you're sitting there, I can't keep my tongue from pressing against these cavities because these holes are new and everything I eat and drink and feel inside them, reminds me of you . . . and I just thought I should say that now . . . and if you want to kiss me good-bye, you can.

My Mother's Eyes

JAMIE PACHINO

KATHLEEN, 25, sits on a doctor's examination table, a white dressing gown on, waiting for the doctor to return.

KATHLEEN: I have my mother's eyes. Everyone tells me. I have her eyes, her waistline, her neck, her ankles. I have some of her jewelry, her taste in shoes, her flair for the dramatic and they even say I drive like her. I have the same pitch in my voice when I get angry, I can get anyone to do something for me with a raised eyebrow—it's a gift—I make lists like her, I give good backrubs, and I waited a long time to lose my virginity, just like she did. But I didn't model myself after her. That just happens when you're a girl. You wind up . . . playing your mother. You model yourself after this woman, because after all, she is the first Woman you know. And you want so badly to be grown up. Of course there's a period where everything she does is wrong, but mostly—you want to be a lady like she is, and know the secrets. I suppose I followed her, and absorbed her, and willed some of her into me, and I have my mother's eyes. But more than anything, I have her taste in men. I looked right at my father and fell in love the first time I saw him, they said. My aunt called it a love affair, and in a strange way it was. It wasn't odd, or strange, or like that—it was just two people who looked at each other and . . . as much as my mother and I look and sound and . . . are . . . alike, there's no getting around the fact that if I had a choice, I would want to be the person my father was.

He was the easiest man I ever knew. He was kind and gentle and very very funny. He had beautiful hazel eyes, droopy, around the corners, and wrinkled, underneath. He had long lashes and high pointy eyebrows and vein roped hands and he was handsome. He had long skinny legs and he played word games with you, and smoked a pipe. He liked that game Mastermind, because he liked things that were logical. He taught me algebra and how to ride a bike, and how to pitch it right into his glove, and he saw the best in people, and I think that was what I wanted the most. To be able to look at a person and think what was good about them, right away, instead of thinking why I shouldn't like them, like my mother did, and why they would disappoint me in the end. I wanted to be more like him in the way that people could surprise me with how nice they were instead of how badly they treated each other.

But instead, I have my mother's eyes. (*She may pick up the stethoscope, other tools, play with them.*)

When I was 16—this is a true story—he sat us down and told us he had this disease. It wasn't serious, he said, it wasn't dire, but it was true. He said that people with his disease—of the kidneys—could live on short doses of dialysis without needing a transplant for something like 15 years, and that if they got a successful one they could live another 15 before things started to break down again, and by that time he was sure this disease would surely have been cured by modern medicine. Because that was the way his world worked. He believed in the world's good nature. My mother was in the room with us. She didn't say anything. I guess she thought differently. Or maybe she just knew better about the way the world worked. I wanted to see things the way he did. And know that things would turn out okay.

He promised me something like 30 years, or a cure from modern medicine, but three years later, when I was 19, he died. Not just—there was the bedridden part, the hospital time, the part where he was poked and needled and catheterized, on a respirator, in that horrible nether world between what he was and what was coming next, the part where he stopped recognizing us, and my mother couldn't pick her head up anymore, but—in the end—failure of the kidneys and he was gone.

And that's when I knew. You know how people never talk about their own death until they're dying? That's how I knew, even at 16, even when he was being so hopeful, that for a man like him to even mention the time when he would be just a body and nothing more, that there wasn't going to be enough time to get out of my mother's body and into his. To grow into his grace and learn what it felt like to be in his skin, instead of her smooth, pale kind, which I inherited along with everything else.

I have it. I have my father's disease. And you know . . . I'm glad. Because now, finally, there's a part of me that belongs to him. I feel . . . closer, I . . . cherish it. Because now I will know something about him, and the way he lived, and the way he died, from this that has nothing to do with anyone else but he and I. I have something that he and I alone share.

I have my mother's eyes. But my father gave me this gift. I know how to look at my life now. Every single day.

Netty's Dance

REGINA PORTER

NETTY, a 50-ish African-American maid who works for an uppercrust African-American family, is in the kitchen preparing dinner.

NETTY: Seems like everybody got something to say 'bout how I do things. Seems like the more I try to do things one way, the more they want to complain. I don't always do things the way they want it done, but the end result is the same. The end result is the same. If I follow these fools up too much, I end up feeling sorry for myself. And that's a bad place to be. I been many things in my life, but sorry for myself is nothing I ever been. Cause if the truth be told, I keep going. *Like the Energizer bunny, baby.* Going and going and going. Sometimes, it's just to pile more food on my plate or to buy groceries for other people's plates. But I'm going. And I can take pleasure in small things, which is more than most can say. Sure, it bothers me every now and again about the flesh that done begun to creep up on my back. The rolls. And I think, Netty, leave that last piece of sweet potato pie in the pan. But as likely as not, ain't no man gone ever see this body nude again. I bathe everyday, and I don't see it. I just kind of pat myself dry with dim eyes. Grateful for a mirror of fog. Which brings me to the heart of the matter: I don't remember a time when I ain't been in my black and white uniform. Granted, my memory ain't what it used to be. Memories blur when you keep going. . . .

Gone Stone Cold

SUSANNA RALLI

MRS. ROSE BURNHAM, an elderly widow in East London, sits at a kitchen table, dressed in a comfortable housedress and flowered apron. On the table are a number of objects: a teapot with a tea cozy on it, two teacups and saucers, a plate of gingersnaps and shortbread, a picture of a man in his 60s set in a silver picture frame, and a rotary telephone. Rose is staring straight ahead of her, looking into space. She frowns in concentration, and absentmindedly sips her tea. At the first sip, she pulls the cup away with a jerk and frowns.

ROSE: Too bloody hot! (*She looks toward the tea setting opposite her on the table and begins to speak.*) Truth be told, I'm not sure what to say, now that I've decided to go ahead with this. How's your tea, love? Hot enough for ya? Good. Lovely. Now you must have a biscuit. You know, I've told the police everything I remember, but I want to tell you what happened. (*Suddenly, Rose pushes the plate of cookies forward, toward her "guest."*) Now you must have a biscuit. My gingersnaps are— were—a particular favorite of my Tom's. Nothing like homemade, he always said. (*Pause*) No, not gingersnaps. Shortbread. You'll have a shortbread. Everyone likes my shortbread. (*Pause*) Why am I babbling on about bloody biscuits? More important things need to be done now.

(*Rose lets go of the plate, and arranges the cups and plate, making everything symmetrical and neat. Then she puts her hand on the telephone, as if she's going to pick up the receiver. But she doesn't. She turns back to her unseen guest and nods, as if he's said something to get her attention.*) Yes. Best get it over with. Like going to the dentist. I'll feel better once it's over. (*Pause*)

It was a Wednesday, teatime. (*She smiles.*) Poor Tom. Poor love. He didn't know what hit him. He walked in the door, just coming from his job down the school. They call him a handyman, but he just mends things really. Does the odd job, here and there. He's retired, of course, but he likes . . . he liked to keep busy. So he walks in and I let him have it. I'd had a hell of a day, brand new boiler on the blink, the baby (*pronounced "babby"*) next door teething and screaming bloody murder. And here comes Tom, walking in the door asking "What's for tea?" I just let him have it, I did, with both barrels. Tea? Just what the bloody hell did he think I did all day, wait for him to come home, so I could make him a cup of bloomin' tea? (*She puts her hand over her mouth and smiles at her "guest" in mock shock at her language.*) Oh dear. I shouldn't swear so much, should I? But I want to tell you everything. Just how it happened. (*She smiles.*)

Now my Tom is an exceptional calm man. Was. There I was, lookin' like murder, and he never raised his voice, or lost his head. He says, "We'll go out tonight, as a treat. Since you work so hard. Makin' my tea and all." And I said, "And the cinema. Fish and chips, and the new Julia Roberts film at the cinema." So we had a bit of supper down at the chippie on the corner—you know Mrs. Bembridge and his wife? Course you do. They make a nice bit of cod, they do. A real treat it was. And then we went down the Marquee and got in line for tickets for the 7 o'clock.

(*Rose stands up and walks to the right a bit. She's obviously agitated. She stares right at her "guest" when she begins to speak, but soon looks away, lost in the vividness of her memories.*) We were standing in line outside a while, ten minutes maybe. There's always a bit of a queue when they've got a new Julia Roberts film. And I remember that the sun was in our eyes, so we turned to look across the square. (*Pause*) And that's when we saw it. This little rucksack, a child's rucksack it was, way over on the other side of the square, on a bench. Course, Tom wanted to go over straight away and get it. But I told him to mind his own business. If the little blighter left it there, and it got stolen, it would teach him a lesson. But Tom—silly bugger—bless him—was always too tenderhearted by half. He kept looking at it. And then he started talking about how the little blighter would get in trouble at home. And what a pretty penny schoolbooks cost these days. And didn't I never make a mistake when I was young? Got married too young, I told him. Should have looked around a bit more. (*She suddenly covers her mouth lightly with her fingers, shocked by what she's said.*) God help me, I said it. I said I got married too young. (*Pause*) Where was I? Right. Then Tom looked at me. Like a spaniel I used to have when I was a little girl. He just stared at me, all pathetic and sadlike. Finally, I couldn't take his expression anymore. I knew we weren't going into the cinema with that bag sitting there, and him thinking of the poor little sod sitting at home, crying that he lost it. (*Rose wanders back to the table and touches the photograph.*) I could never say no to him when he looked at me that way. (*Long pause. Rose looks away into space, remembering.*) So I says, "Go ahead then and get the bag and take it to Lost Property in the cinema." And he took off like a shot, before I'd even finished speaking. I saw him across the square, picking up that little rucksack like it was the Holy Grail. Big smile on his face. Soft bloody fool. (*Long pause. Rose looks away into space, remembering.*)

People nowadays don't remember what it was like during the war. They think the worst part of the bombing was all noise and explosions. Shell shock, they called it. But I always thought the worst part was just after the bombs dropped. The terrible quiet, like it was the end of the world. It wasn't so bad in the shelters, but sometimes people didn't make it to the shelters. There's a blast of light and sound, and then nothing. You can't hear anything. No voices, no birds, not even your own breathing. You can't see anything through the smoke. Like it's night. You can't feel anything. You can hardly breathe. You're not sure if you're alive or dead. So you wait. And just when you think you might be dead, you realize your heart's beating, so you must be alive.

And then the sounds start to come back. There's a funny sound. You don't recognize it at first. You think it might be human, but you've never heard a person make that kind of sound before. It's the sound of pain. Sounds more like an animal than a person. But it's not just the pain what makes them scream like that—it's the horror. When they come to and find they're trapped in a grave of soil and stone. When they reach to pull themselves out of the rubble, and realize they don't have a left hand anymore. (*Rose clenches her fist.*) Or you turn to your sister, your little sister, and you find you're holding the blue cardigan what your mother knitted last Christmas, but she's not in it anymore. It's like she's just disappeared off the face of the earth. (*Pause. Rose unclenches her fist. She looks quickly at the telephone, then apologetically at her "guest."*)

I'm not doing very well, am I? And there's not a lot of time, is there? Well, Tom always said, practice makes perfect. So I'll keep going. Where was I? Ah, so there I was next to the Marquee. Lying there. And I knew there were people who needed help. But all I could think of was getting over to that bloody bench and seeing what had happened to Tom. But Tom was gone. There was no bag. There was no bench. There was no pavement. No Tom. (*Pause*)

I remember Mum, sitting next to me in the shelter. And she was holding my hand, and I could feel her shaking. I thought she was afraid, like the others. I thought she was afraid of what had happened. What might happen next. I thought she was crying. I was going to say something to comfort her. But when I looked up at her, I didn't see fear. It was anger. She was so angry that she was shaking with the force of it, a mighty wave of hate welling up in her. And as I held my mother's hand, it felt so cold. Trembling, and stone cold. I can tell you, if Hitler had been in our little shelter on Crowley Street that night, the war would have been over a hell of a lot sooner. (*Pause. She smiles wryly at her "guest." She picks up the framed picture, and turns it toward her guest.*)

Look at him. Look at that sweet face. He did his duty, he

served his time for his country. They gave him a special pin for bravery, and he'd wear it all the time, that's how proud he was. But he never killed anyone. Never hurt a soul in his whole life. And those cowards killed him. Blotted him out like he meant nothing. Like all his goodness didn't count for anything. They didn't even have the nerve to face us—just left the bomb behind and ran off. Terrorists, they call them. Cowards, I say. And the police say they have no leads. That these are professionals and they don't leave a trace. But by God everybody leaves a trace. (*Aside*) Those bastards have to eat. They have to sleep. They have to travel. They have faces.

(*Rose stands next to the table and grips the side with clenched fingers. She looks straight at her "guest," and speaks very distinctly and carefully.*) I've tried praying. I've gone to church. I've talked to the vicar. All he tells me is that Tom's in a better place. A happy place. But what about me? I've tried crying. But my eyes stay dry, and all I feel is the cold. So cold. That's why I need your help. You must help me! (*Pause, she taps her fingers on her lips, concentrating, then pulls them away.*) Your Auntie Gwynn gave me your number, Patrick. She's told me a lot about you. Oh no, not details or anything, just how you know about these things. That you know how to find people. What to do. I've sort of filled in the gaps myself, so to speak. (*Suddenly she leans forward, and looks intensely into her "guest's" eyes.*)

You must understand something, I don't give a rat's arse about politics. I don't care which God people worship. And I don't care why people kill. But my Tom was a good kind man and they killed him, and someone has to pay for it. I do have some money put aside, and it's all yours. (*Suddenly, her expression turns very blank and very cold.*) It's all yours, Patrick, if you find the people who planted that bomb and blow their fucking heads off. Will you do it for me? Please.

(*Rose sighs hard. She sits down and closes her eyes for a moment. Then she opens them and picks up the framed photograph. She stares at it long and hard. Suddenly, she puts down the photograph, stands up, and walks a few steps away from the table.*

She shouts back at the picture.) Dear God, man, stop looking at me like that. I want justice. I want to . . . Stop looking at me! (*Suddenly, she bursts into tears. She covers her face, and turns away from the table. After a few moments, she calms down, and sits back down at the table. She picks up the photograph, smiling sadly.*) You're never coming back, my dear, are you? And there's nothing I can do to get you back.

(*Rose puts down the photo. She picks up the phone and dials a number.*) Hello, Gwynnie. Not so bad, love. Better than yesterday. Yeah, I said I'd ring you this morning. But . . . nothing important. I was going to ask if that nice nephew of yours—what's his name, Patrick?—if he would help me put away some of Tom's things. But I think I can look after it myself. (*Pause, then she continues in a forced, cheerful voice.*) I've got to run, love. (*She whistles into the phone.*) Kettle's whistlin'. Ta ta, I'll ring you soon. (*She hangs up the phone. With a sigh, she picks up the photograph and places it, facing her, at the opposite end of the table, next to the other place setting. Then she picks up her "guest's" teacup and sips the cold tea. She makes a face.*) Stone bloody cold. (*She stares straight out ahead of her, emotionless, looking just as she did in the beginning of the scene.*)

Circus Madness

JACQUELYN REINGOLD

A woman with her arms up over her head as if she's holding onto a trapeze swing.

The thing is. The thing is. About letting go. Which is what I'm thinking about. Letting go. Is. The thing is. I don't know who put up the net today. I don't know who tied the knots. Was it Cannon Ball Bill, the former Eagle Scout, best knot maker under the tent? That would be safe. That would good. Or was it Sukee the Russian Contortionist who found me with her lover, Enrique O'Reilly the ringmaster, in his bed? Did she hang that net? That would be bad. Or maybe it was Porgy Alonso, the fish trainer, he's always good with a net. Then again, worst of all, it could have been Pepe the evil clown. Known best for making children of all ages cry, and having stabbed his ex-wife Winona, the sword swallower, to death. Or could it even have been Enrique O'Reilly the ring-master himself, who, through no fault of his own, is well known for his—slippery fingers. Oh Enrique, you should never have gone back to Sukee the Contortionist's bed. While I understand the appeal of a woman who can put her legs above her head, with me you could have flown, we could have soared. Alas. I wonder who tied the damn net today.

If I knew I'd let go. But best to hold on. And on. 'Cause you never know. What's below.

Except except. I'm tired. Awfully tired. Unbearably tired. Terribly tired. Exhausted, weary, tuckered out, spent kind of tired. And my arms. My arms. Are killing me. I am dying from the pain in my arms. It never gets any easier. And it would be ever so sweet to drop them flop them and fall down

down down. Then do that bounce that I love, that spring, that lope. Bottom-up! Bottom-up. Bottom-up. The crowd cheers. You're dead, you're alive, you're saved. They give you a special meal. Steak. Or duck. Or veal.

But no, better not. 'Cause what about that net? And what might be below? A soft bed? A bath tub? A pile of manure? Besides, what would Mario do, when he comes flying my way trying to catch himself on my ankles, and I'm not there. He'd fall, too.

But if only. Ow. I could only. Ow. Drop them. Even one. The right or the left, left or right. Just one. Better not. I guess. (*She drops her right arm.*) Oh relief, oh blessed God, it's good. My right arm. It is good. Ah. Ow. But now the left is hurting even worse. Oh. Ow. (*She puts them both up again. She drops left arm.*) Oh. Yes. The left. But now the right one is even worse. (*Both arms up.*)

Nothing to do. Think about elves. Or Enrique. Or how to do the mambo. Or how cold is it today. Why do washing machines last so long? Why do dryers always break? How come I always hate the tightrope walkers and like the elephant trainers? If I keep trying could I get my legs behind my head?

I wonder what's for lunch today. I hope it's not chicken. I am so sick of chicken. I will kill myself if it's chicken.

The thing is. About letting go. Is. I don't know who put up the net today. But maybe I don't care. (*She drops her arms.*)

Variations on a Theme

TANIA RICHARD

*NADINE, a black actress, is rehearsing a monologue with her the-
ater company. When she performs the monologue, she speaks in a
deep, old-fashioned, southern accent.*

NADINE: I been singin' all my life. It's rumored I sang befo' I
talked. My Granmama says I sang my first word. (*She sings.*)
Liberty! (*She speaks.*) Give me liberty or give me death! Ain't
that how the sayin' goes? I like the sound of that! (*She stops
suddenly. In her own voice.*) Sorry. (*Takes a moment. Starts
again in a southern accent.*) I've been singin' all my life. It's
rumored that I sang befo' I talked. My Granmama says I sang
my first word. (*Half-heartedly, she sings.*) Liberty! (*Speaks, slowly. She is running out of steam.*) Give me li-ber-ty or—(*In her
own voice. She is addressing the director and playwright sitting in
the rehearsal room.*) I can't do this, I need a new fuckin' character. I've been playing the same damn character for five years.
Sassy black girl, who can sing! First, there was Nellie, in *Justice
for a Black World.* She could sing, she was sassy, she was black!
Then, there was Aretha in *That Girl Can Sing.* What do you
think she was like? Hmmmm? She was black, she sure was
sassy, and damn, she could sing! Then there was Vera,
Veronica, on and on. You want to know what I want? I want
to be in a goddamn play where I don't have to sing one damn
note! Where I'm as submissive and unsassy as Laura in *The
Glass Menagerie,* or as bitchy as Martha in *Who's Afraid of
Virginia Woolf*! Don't get me wrong, Clarice, you are a great
writer, but for God's sake, write something else! Anything else!
What about today? What's going on today? Sister to Sister.
Brother to Brother. If I never read another play about blacks

in the nineteen thirties, or forties, or whenever, ever again, it will be too damn soon! Haven't we as a people done anything other than, sing, dance, and act sassy? Surely, we have done something else!

Qualification 2

KATE ROBIN

BECKY *is an attractive woman in her late 20s with large round breasts.*

BECKY: The funny thing is that I always thought I had this really hot body. I mean, when other women bitched about being too fat or whatever, I never felt that way. I knew it wasn't perfect, but I really felt it was nice . . . and I always liked being naked, you know, I was happy to have sex with the lights on. Men seemed to like it. Then I started seeing Mitch—my partner, I mean, and he had all these issues with . . . well, you know, sex, I guess. He couldn't really, sometimes he could, but most of the time, he couldn't get an erection? And after it happened a few times he said maybe it was because I wasn't really his "type" physically. Because I have such small breasts? And at first I just thought that was ridiculous, because, you know, no one else had ever had a problem with them. Then he said something about how he didn't usually go for brunettes. By the way, his mother is this incredibly voluptuous bottle blonde. Fat, really, she's fat. But anyway, it went on like this—with him saying he was in *love* with me, but there just seemed to be something wrong with the way I looked. Not that I wasn't attractive, but just somehow, not his thing. So, first I lightened my hair, of course. Because you know, at a certain point, who doesn't? Then I started noticing other women's breasts. They all looked so much bigger and more luscious than mine. I sort of couldn't believe I'd never noticed before how . . . depleted I was in this area, or how much men really cared about this. It seemed like all the men I'd ever had sex with must have just been very nice to act as though I had a nice body when obviously, they must have been horribly disappointed by my sad little tiny breasts. Well, I guess it's pretty obvious what I did next. (*She indicates her large, unnaturally round and perky breasts.*) And, you know for a few weeks he was really into it, but then it just wore off or something. (*Pause*) I used to think there were a million ways to be beautiful, now it seems impossible. And every mark, every scar or mole on my body, every stray hair now, is like a betrayal. Like that's the thing that made this happen to me. The reason I can't be happy. I used to be the only woman I knew who loved her body. Now, I'm just like everyone else.

Excerpt from *The Clean House*

SARAH RUHL

VIRGINIA is a woman in her 50s who loves to clean.

VIRGINIA: People who give up the *privilege* of cleaning their own houses—they're insane people. If you do not clean, how do you know if you've made any progress in life? I love dust. The dust always makes progress. Then I remove the dust. That is progress. If it were not for dust I think I would die. If there were no dust to clean then there would be so much leisure time and so much thinking time and I would have to do something besides thinking and that thing might be to slit my wrists. Ha ha ha ha ha ha just kidding. I'm not a morbid person. That just popped out!

My sister is a wonderful person. She's a doctor. At an important hospital. I've always wondered how one hospital can be more important than another hospital. They are places for human waste. Places to put dead bodies. I'm sorry. I'm being morbid again.

My sister has given up the privilege of cleaning her own house. Something deeply personal—she has given up. She does not know how long it takes the dust to accumulate under her bed. She does not know if her husband is sleeping with a prostitute because she does not smell his dirty underwear. All of these things, she fails to know.

I know when there is dust on the mirror. Don't misunderstand me—I'm an educated woman. If I were to die at any moment during the day, no one would have to clean my kitchen.

Excerpt from *Under Yelena*

BUFFY SEDLACHEK

RUTA speaks to her comrade as the Soviet Union is falling.

RUTA: I have worked within the party to outdistance weakness, to be an equal member of this society—-for what? Opportunity snatched away?!! Reduced to a weeping Ukrainian woman at the height of my career?!? This is not cause for celebration, my friend, this is the end of my life. (*Pause*)

The day my brother is born. I'm watching my father run to the river. Laughing wildly he's plunging my newborn brother into the icy waters of the Dnieper. He is very drunk and yelling. "The river makes us strong—or we sink! The river gives us life—or we drown! This is the way to prepare for living! Your grandfather plunged me, and I plunge your brother, Rutala." My baby brother—he goes into the rushing water helpless and small. "When we survive the river, we are STRONG. Nothing else can ever be as difficult. . . . Nothing worse can happen to us. This is the wisdom of the fathers, and the grandfathers back through time, Rutala."

I'm asking my father how cold was the river on my day of birth. When I was being plunged. And he is laughing. "We do not give this strength to our daughters! Rutala, Rutala, use your head!"

And at night. I tie my ankles to a rope. I tie the rope to a tree. And . . . I plunge myself into the strongest current of the river. It is very cold. I have killed myself. I am sure of this. And pulling hand over hand over hand, up the rope, against the current, taking in tremendous gulps of water, I am fighting back to the land. And, there is my father, and my drunken uncles and they are laughing. The stinking drunken men of my family, all laughing. But I am six years old. And I am strong; no matter how they laugh. . . . Nothing worse can ever happen to me. Nothing worse.

I take my life into my own hands. And this is where it leads? In the party I am called a comrade. An equal. And Rutala is dead with the laughter of my father. I cannot go back, I will not go back.

The Black Eyed

BETTY SHAMIEH

TAMAM, a woman in her early 30s, is trying to convince a chorus of women to help her search for her brother.

My name is Tamam. It means enough. I was called that because my family wanted no more daughters. I am the last of seven sisters, good luck for the family. After me, there were two brothers and now there is only one. Why do we rejoice when a boy is born?

Because we from Gaza understand the power of might. The strong make the rules, name the cities, and decide who live in them, or so they think. We know what it means to be weak, to cement a settlement of resentment, brick by brick, in our own ravaged hearts and shell-shocked minds, with every corner littered with bullets, tear gas canisters, that say "Made in Pennsylvania" on them. Times like these call for soldiers. The ones we had have fallen. . . .

I want to talk about something smaller than me that became bigger. I want to talk about my brother. He was caught with a rock in his hand and a curse on his lips. I went to the jail to visit my brother. Most of my people looked at the Israeli guards, with every ounce of hatred a human heart can hold, their faces twisted not like they tasted something bitter, like something bitter was forced down their throats. I was smarter than that. I knew I must navigate through the maze of might, and did my best to be kindly, polite. Hoping perhaps that I would remind them of a Rachel or Sarah or Ruth that they knew or would have liked to know. So when they beat my brother, that thing that started out smaller than me and got bigger, they would lighten their touch. And I smiled my best smile when the soldiers opened the gate for me. Weighed down with baskets of food, I brought extra, hoping to create the illusion that that dirty jail was one place were there was enough and extra for all the guards to eat twice. Otherwise, my brother would get none. Unless there was enough and extra. They thanked me for the food and they raped me in front of him, forcing my brother's eyes open so he had to watch. They wanted to know something that he preferred not to tell them. They skewered the support for their argument into my flesh.

I'm told that their torture specialists who study the "Arab" mind realized rape would enrage our men. Enraging a man is the first step on the stairway that gets him to a place where he becomes impotent, helpless. They not only refer to us as the cockroaches, they examine us, experiment upon us, as if we were that predictable, that much the same, that easy to eradicate. Their studies show the Arab men value the virtue of their womenfolk. Their studies show something within me was supposed to be inviolate. Say what you want about Arab men and women and how we love one another, there is one thing that's for certain. There are real repercussions for hurting a woman in my society. There are repercussions.

When the first hand was laid upon me, we both screamed. The evolutionary function of a scream is a cry for help, they tied down the only one who could so I silenced myself. That was the only way to tell my brother I didn't want him to tell. I flinched when I had to, but I kept my breathing regular. My brother tried to look every other way, but realized I needed him, to look me in the eyes and understand. They thought making us face one another in our misery would break us. But we were used to misery. It's like anything else, you can build up a tolerance for it.

Someone else told them what they wanted to know, so they released my brother two weeks later. That's when he built something more intricate than the human heart, hugged it to his chest, and boarded a bus that was going nowhere and everywhere. Listen, I don't agree with killing innocent people under any circumstances, ever. The irony is there were Palestinians who were Israeli citizens on that bus too. My brother wasn't counting on that. No one was counting on that. I should have known what my brother was bound to do, I could have stopped him. I said every time he went out to face their guns with our rocks. "Don't go. Let's achieve peace by peaceful means. Let's use non-violence. Don't be a pawn. What kind of fool would face a gun with a rock? Let others risk their lives. They can never truly win. They could kill every Palestinian and the wind will howl our names and the rocks will rise up and throw themselves." I'd always say "Don't go." But I didn't say "You are the most precious thing in the world to me. The fact that you exist makes the earth spin on its axis, it's rolling for joy because you are here. The sun shows up to see you, and the moon chases the sun off to be in your sky and none of them love you like I do, brother. Not even close. . . ."

My name is Tamam. It means enough.

God Is A Dyke

JANE SHEPARD

JESSIE walks out on stage. She is a young woman in a leather jacket, bandana, and big boots. Very Brooklyn.

JESSIE: Whoa. I dunnow if you ever done this, stood up on a stage like this, but it's very, very weird. Can't see shit! (*Signifies stage wings.*) An' that . . . space . . . very weird, what is that for? I feel like little elves are gonna come out or somethin'. (*In Munchkin voice*) "Come out, come out, wherever you are . . ."

Well, I came out. No pun intended. "An' now a very nice dyke will come out an' discuss her philosophy." Yeah, right! I'm afraid I got very little to share on this subject. An' what I do know, you prob'ly heard already. An if you ain't heard it, you prob'ly didn't care to know it in the first place. An' if you don't know it an' you *do* care, ya prob'ly wouldn't understand it, an' if ya *do* an' ya *do*, who the fuck knows what you're talkin' about anyhow?!

So putz with the philosophy. "Never poke a stick up a dog's ass." There's with your philosophy. Or, no, wait a minnit . . . ! (*Jessie gets a garbage can from the side of the stage, emptying out the trash carelessly.*) Oo, they shoulda never turned me loose! (*She pulls a jumbo marker out of her jacket and writes on the can.*) "SHIT HAPPENS." There! Da Da! (*Shows it.*) Whaddya think? Does this cover the philosophical map or what! Anybody feel left out? This is great. This covers the spectrum. "Hey, babe, you lost your wallet? I got a spare hundred, take it, shit happens." "Yo, weege, your friend, never paid me back, hadda take his thumbs, y'know, shit happens." (*She smiles at audience, on a roll now.*) This, I think, is why the Bible is so big. Plays it both ways. "Turn the other cheek" an'

"Eye for an eye" under the same cover. Very handy! Whichever way ya wanna play it. My sister-in-law, she's Catholic, no wonder she's schizophrenic, right? God: the judgmental father, Jesus: compulsively forgiving son, very conflicted family!

Whoa. I digress. Royally. I should chill. Do a little meditation. I know this chick, right, she's Buddhist? Most cool lady, very righteous, in body as well as mind, a body I would not kick outta my bed, let me not lie, even if I do digress, the woman makes me want to moan, faint an' die! Nonetheless, her philosophy, very close to "Shit Happens." So no wonder she got peace, what's to argue? Whaddya gonna say, don't chant so loud? Don't meditate so close to the shrubbery?

'Course, I dunnow how they do when the shit hits the fan. I never seen a Buddhist on the battle field. "Joe, Joe, we're goin' on patrol! You wanna come?" "Yeah, gimmie a minute to meditate." "Joe, Joe, they blew your leg off! You wanna meditate?" "Fuck no, kill all those motherfuckers!" It's when it gets rough, you start to find out what you really believe, right? All of a sudden how you look at it becomes very important. What you choose. How you see yourself. I mean, say, for the sake of example . . .

(*Gets garbage can.*) This is you. (*She touches its shape.*) Very nice, got your own individuations, a nick here or there, but basically, very smooth. (*Lays can on its side.*) You roll into life. (*She rolls it.*) Very nice. There you are. Now, I, for this sophisticated demonstration, will represent . . . (*Brings hammer from backstage.*) . . . Life! (*Goes to can.*) There are certain occurrences of life, that shape you . . . (*She looks at the garbage can with intent.*) Say, bus accident . . . (*Raises hammer.*) No. Not a accident. Somethin' more . . . significant. Human nature. The look. The touch. The incident. The silence in the room. That does this to you . . . (*With a sudden violent vehemence, she stomps the can a good one with her boot, leaving the barrel dented and misshapen.*) Okay. Now we have effect. Something has occurred. An' from now on . . . (*Jessie pushes the garbage can, it rolls unevenly.*) . . . You will not move through life the same. You ain't never gonna go back, that's just the shape a you now.

So. Now it gets tricky. The real quest begins. Sooner or later you gonna have to decide. Are you permanently damaged? Or will you merely roll differently? Myself, I don't care. I got no answers. Whatever gets ya through the night, as Janis Joplin said. Some people got God. Some got destiny, or philosophy, or botany, although I dunnow what that is, but it's bugs or somethin'. And some people got the philosophy a pokin' holes in other people's philosophy. "Sure, Jessie, you love God, but if you gonna live that 'lifestyle,' don't expect him to love you back!" Well fine, if God is some big old straight guy up there, that would explain a lot! But maybe he ain't. Who's to say? Maybe God's my neighbor in Brooklyn, hears the term "oral sex" for the first time in her 85 years, says, "It's all good." Or maybe God is me in a leather jacket! Ain't nothin' makes me feel more heavenly than this! And by the way, lemme tell ya, if God is a dyke, ain't one'a you gettin' into heaven without much, much better boots! Boots & jacket, totally divine. Eight years I been wearin' this, since when I come out as a lesbian. Yeah, that's right, you gotta say the word. Lesbian! Big Dyke. God or no God. Sin or no sin. Life or death. You are what you are, and if you ain't, you got no life anyway.

But you get lucky enough to meet somebody, a person what makes your heart sing, I don't care *who* it is, you better walk that walk! An' lemme tall ya, baby, we did! Walk it, dance it, me & Sharon, we done every dyke march since we been together! Day before the pride parade. Demonstrated our asses off in Washington! Once, we're marchin' by, Sharon drops trou right on the street an' moons her white ass right at the White House! Ha! They didn't even notice. I noticed. Go to all the parties, gay & lesbian center, very excellent dancer, oo, I just stand by like, "Is she incredible?! She mine!" Got the tattoos, sixth anniverary. Last year, domestic partnership, city a New York, wearin' yours truly, thank you very much.

Last summer, we was sittin' in the diner, Seventh Avenue, Park Slope, man comes in, stops at our table, says, "Know how I knew you was lezzies? The leather jackets." He lifts up his arm, an' he's got a baseball bat. I see Sharon's eyes get real big, and I start to stand up, an' I hear this thunk. An' suddenly I'm lyin' on the wet linoleum, an' I got a helluva headache, an' I'm thinkin', "Somethin' about this is not right." An' I hear this sound. There's this *absolute silence* in the room. An' in it, I hear this thunk! Thunk! Thunk! And it sounds to me like somebody puttin' dents in a garbage can. An' I just can't figure out why I'm lyin' on the floor an' somebody's poundin' dents in a garbage can. An' then I see this blood on the linoleum, runnin' towards me. An' I'm thinkin', "It's such a shame. It's gonna stain the jacket, an' I can't get outta the way."

Life becomes very, very lonely, in that moment. You don't feel like no big tough dyke. You feel like just some little six year old, stained your dress, an' now you can't get outta the way. There is no philosophy for this time. You are alone. You can't make that sound stop. An' it ain't never gonna change back. No matter what you do. You only get to go on. Very tricky. One of these very tricky times, findin' a way to go on. I mean, you do go on. But to . . . go forward . . . in life . . . (*She struggles a moment, stranded onstage.*) I mean, here we are right now, an' I don't even wanna go forward from here. I, I, I could leave this stage right now, actually. An' you'd all be sittin' here goin', "What the fuck was that?!" Right? "What the hell kind of a story is that to tell?! You should just stick to talkin' to cans," right?

(*Looks at can.*) They ain't never caught him. Everybody was so stunned, they said. He just walked right out. In the silence. Walkin' around now. You can see where a specific take on things would come of assistance. Lil' philosophy. 'Cause you gonna have a time like this, see, sooner or later, when all them things what make the world make sense don't mean jack shit. All in a flash, no more. Thunk. What'dya got then, y'know? "Shit happens"?

I got 52 stitches. Got a scar that people envy when they're comparin' scars. The hearin' loss they don't envy, left hand still not so hot, and I got a voice runnin' in my head, oh yeah, I got a voice talkin' to me all the time tellin' me this man should *not be free*. An' it is not wise to walk around, come in public, with these things in your head, better you should go to synagogue an' pray, but this is tricky also, because every minute you find yourself prayin', "God, just lemme find the guy, lemme just once meet this fuck on a dark street, this man, who beat a woman to death with a bat!"

Not a dyke in a leather jacket, who's lyin' right there in front of you, but a school teacher, just turned 34, who was reachin' down to me, that's all, just reachin' out with her gentle hands, and he— She don't even wear the jacket except on weekends, she don't take it to school 'cause kids need somebody they look up to and who respects 'em an' looks nice just for 'em, in class, because they count, an' who wears . . . who wears a little bit a perfume, just a little bit, jaw line an' wrist, very delicate wrist, so they see how a little bit a scent, just for yourself, shows self-respect. Won't even go to brunch before 12:30 on Sunday 'cause she gotta go to church an' talk to God. "Bye, Jessie, see ya in a bit, gotta go talk with God!" An' if God is listenin' right now he's hearin' me say, "Go fuck yourself!" 'Cause nobody deserves to be believed in who lets that happen. She was the kind of person we needed on this earth! Not me, I wouldn'a mind I died! I was right there, he should'a took me, I got nothin' more to offer this world anyhow. I got no more songs in my heart, sorry, Sharon, but it's true. This can is completely flat!

(*She stomps the can.*) I wish to God you was here, honey, 'cause you would'a known what to do. You would still be standin', you'd a rose above it an' said, "I will not be stopped." Her hands would be reachin' out still, goin', "Don't worry honey, I'm here, an' I am gonna lift you up! (*She lifts the can above her head.*) I will lift you and show you to a world where people murder with a bat!" An' you would say, "By the power of love in me, you fuckin' sons of bitches, if you wanna stop me, it will take more than *dents!*" (*Jessie slams the can down.*) An' if God don't stand for that, then God *will* be a dyke in a leather jacket! A great big, fat lesbian in the sky who will raise us above this *mess!* And you would say, like you did a long time ago when I told you I couldn't make love, "It's up to you. Are you permanently damaged, or will you merely roll differently?"

(*Silence. She stands alone.*) Well I'm not God. An' Sharon ain't here. An' I would give anything, anything her blue eyes was still lookin' on this world. But it's just me. An' I will not be stopped. If we truly don't get no say about what happens . . . If all we get is how we look at it, then somehow, some way . . . (*She looks out.*) . . . we all gonna need much, much better boots.

(*She stands a moment, looking out, no longer nervous.*) Well, I gotta get off this stage now. (*Looks at smashed can, glances offstage.*) Somebody's gonna be really pissed. You see somebody later, they ask you what the fuck happened to their trash can, just look 'em in the eye and say, "So what? Now it just rolls different." Yeah. (*Jessie smiles, turns, and walks off the stage, leaving the can where it is.*)

The Shaman on the Mountain

LILLIAN ANN SLUGOCKI

A nude woman, with a sheet loosely draped over her body, stands alone in a pool of light.

Last night, my lover fell asleep on the couch. We were at his best friend's cabin, up in the mountains. It was still early, so his best friend and I walked out around the lake by the mountain to visit the local shaman who has a cave, a holy place. A place where visions are born. "Look. You sit here. In the center. And the shaman heats up rocks outside the cave and brings them inside. The temperature rises to 105 degrees centigrade. You sweat and sweat until visions of your totem fill your head."

But, the shaman is nowhere to be seen and the night is really black and the trees are shaking in the breeze and the mountain is silent and the angled beauty of Cassiopeia cuts the night sky—I say: "Look. Up there. Like a bolt of lightning. That's Cassiopeia, the queen. And that bright star there, to the south is Sirius, the dog star." Then his best friend puts his arm around me because I'm barefoot and drunk and the night is really black and who the hell wants to fall in the lake or get lost in the cave—then he says: "I can't believe how beautiful you are." He starts stroking my hair and I realize, not without some despair, that I am crazy again.

We get back to the house as the sun is coming up, and I'm mixing white wine with red wine and he's still stroking the back of my hair when the other man, my lover, wakes up and walks into the kitchen wearing white underpants and a t-shirt, and he says: "Remember me? Remember me, baby?" So I end up in bed with him which is where I'm supposed to be anyway. The jeans come off, the t-shirt, the black brassiere, and last but not least—the ridiculous ruffled panties. He pulls on a condom and it's like a white flag waving at me from the edge of the bed. "We're gonna do it," he says.

Later that morning my lover and his best friend go down to the lake to fish—they've both been avoiding me all morning. It's just as well because I'm still in love with my ex-husband. I sit on the porch and watch the wind move the grass and the leaves on the trees and that same hawk continues to circle the sky over my head. Over and over and over until the symbol for infinity reveals itself, until the shaman lumbers up the hill with an eighteen-inch wide-mouth bass strung from a hook, but I don't tell him I entered his cave last night. I admire his fish and revel in the intimate knowledge of his holy place high up in the mountains: "You know me. You do. I've been to your cave at dawn. I let a stranger stroke the back of my neck, and my long blonde hair until a song sprung from my lips."

Excerpt from *Slow Fast Walking on the Red Eye*

CARIDAD SVICH

CLAUDIA encounters her ex-lover on a tropical island. This is the first time she reveals herself and confronts him without a disguise.

CLAUDIA: You would ignore me for days. I'd wound myself to see if you'd notice. Small cuts on my arms, legs. You never said anything. You'd leave old postcards on a tray, and say "These are for you. Read them. I must run now." And I would. Dutifully. I'd look at the postcards with pictures of trails on them, historic sites that no longer exist, and think, "Oh. He wants me to study these. So I can remember to value things before they're gone. How damn thoughtful of him." I told you about my rage. You never listened. You said, "Lay off the spliff." I said, "I don't do spliff. That must be someone else. I only do ecstasy. And goddamn placebos that make me smile." I'd get dressed up for a party. I'd put on a red silk chemise, and you'd kiss me on the cheek, and let everyone else look at me. But you wouldn't look. You were wrapped up in deals, in meaningless transactions that you hoped would someday turn you a profit because you wanted those dot.com boys to acknowledge you, even if they were the kind to lose a friend over a web site. You wanted to be a part of something: the mobile world, and thus have complete control of your imme-diate landscape. I'd slip away onto a terrace, a deck, a balcony while you mixed in the party's swirl. And I tried to breathe. Well, I couldn't do it anymore. You want blame, take it, take all of it. Live with it, Stewart. Pretend you're someone else, disguise yourself, you won't escape me. Not even here in the tropics where you think the sun will save you. I'll follow you. I'll bite your wrists and cut you open—again and again. I will take your tongue. And then I will give it back to you, and you will be un-moored and remember bits of religion, of faith that you have kept buried for fear of showing it to anyone. And you will kiss me, as if saying good-bye, but I will find you in different shapes: as a man, a woman, a bird held in someone's hand . . . and you will keep wanting to be near me. Go on. Have a drink. It's sweet, like a liquid sugar cube. It will go straight into your veins, and sustain you on the most delirious high. You'll squat anywhere. Under a palm tree, in Waterloo. Pavement and rocks will fall away as you soar at an altitude of twenty-five feet above gray water on the sheerest of unseen wings. Sugar will enter every part of your being until you can't think. About anything. Except me. That's what you want, isn't it? No one else but me? Go on, then. Drink.

God Is Kind to Some Women

C. DENBY SWANSON

SOLACE, a female performance artist in her 20s with a penchant for fresh vegetables, has been conscripted into a different business by an undercover, cross-dressing secret service agent.

SOLACE: It all started at the juice bar. Wheat grass for the lady, he ordered. Make it a double. Later, there would be nettle tea and cold filtered water, but at that moment, in the immediacy of that particular moment I was intoxicated by fresh pulp. Had just come off a swing shift at the grocery store. Stocking produce, my hands still sticky with sap and seeds. He wore women's clothes, he said, because he couldn't be true to anyone else so he had to be true to himself. Truth! I thought he was an artist. Wilson. I betrayed a friendship in exchange for an afternoon of blue green algae. He asked me questions. He played me, he played me like a lute. (*Giddily aside.*) A lute is a *pear*-shaped instrument.

Before I knew it, he was my confidante, my trusted advisor, my looking glass, and I was his informant. Sidled up between a man and my glass of pastoral bliss, I informed on a friendship. She was the kind of person who ordered 10 CD's for a penny and then canceled her membership. Then she ordered 10 CD's for a penny for her cat, and canceled its membership. She did this a number of times and I did not condone her behavior. It irked me for all kinds of social justice reasons, it betrayed the free-market values which comprise every American's circle of stones, their holy place. This friend had, after all, signed a contract. And I told him that. Wilson

128

and I, we laughed about it, ha ha this act of suburban subversion. He and I laughed about it and meanwhile he bought another round of field frolic before I could come down from the first. He asked me what else did I know. I got the spins. He downed his shot of spirulina and turned his glass over on the unbleached wood of the bar. I did not show up for work the next day.

When the feds raided my friend, her small efficiency apartment overrun the following week, they confiscated forged music preference surveys and 12,860 compact disks, some of which contained explicit lyrics.

I'll Never Be Skinny Again

FIONA J. TORRES

The speaker is a pregnant Hispanic woman, 20s.

Don't tell nobody what I'm about to tell you. Promise? I am having a baby. Tony, my husband, tells me, Felicia, do you really think you can keep it a secret? I say, you just watch me. I am going to sit in this house for nine months, and when I come out, I am going to be skinny. He just laughs. He tells me, Felicia, the way you eat, you'll never be skinny again. I say, hey, Panzon, the way you drink, you'll never be skinny, either. You should see him with the belly hanging out like this. It's all the beer he drinks. You'd think he was the one having the baby. He hugs me and grabs my chee-chehs, and says, I like a woman with some pechos. Let me see your pechos. I say, oh, no, you can't see nothing. That's how this whole thing started. He wanted to see my pechos. Just let me see, he said. I only want a little peek. Well, he peeked, and he peeked, and you know what happened. I got pregnant. Oh, we were in love and all that. We got married. When I was real big, my abuela came to see me. My grandmother, God bless her, had ten children. That was before my grandfather died. I was telling her how happy me and Tony were and so glad about the baby and all that, and you know what she said? She said, mi hija, before this is over, you will curse your husband. I said, abuelita, I love my husband. I will never curse him. Let me tell you, one week later, when I was in that delivery room pushing my guts out, I understood what she meant, and I cursed him. Well, this time, I ain't gonna wait no nine months. This time I curse him NOW, and I will never let him see my pechos again. If this keeps up, I swear, I'll never be skinny again.

Fruit Flies

JENNIE WEBB

A somewhat righteous woman speaks directly to the audience.

JESSICA: I'm a vegetarian. I don't eat meat and I don't wear leather. I have had more pets in my lifetime than I can now remember, although at one point I could recite all their names alphabetically—and it was over a hundred then. Yes, I've sprayed paint on furs in Beverly Hills. I only buy cruelty-free products and I read labels diligently, always on the lookout for animal ingredients. Animal experimentation? I've been arrested three times.

Okay. Some of you may think I'm nuts but . . . please! Think of how many times you've looked at a dog or a cat or a rabbit or—you know—I mean, right in the eyes, and they understand! And if that hasn't happened to you, you can just leave or whatever . . . or stay . . . but you may not really understand the point of what I wanted to tell you.

It's these fruit flies.

Now I am not an un-clean person. I am actually quite tidy. I don't leave rotting fruit or—god forbid—rotting flesh lying around and my condo has good ventilation . . . so I . . . I don't understand! Why these . . . these little . . . I tried to reason with them! But there are—my lord—thousands of them! Swarms of them! People say it's because of the heat. What heat? And because of the humidity. Okay. But it's like . . . it's like they know who they're dealing with, right? And . . . At first, when they started . . . gathering . . . I just opened my door. Left it open. I felt sorry for them trapped inside. And then I would take out the trash—once, then twice, then three or four or more times a day. Then on the hour. But they came back. And, you know, it wasn't a new batch, it was the same ones. I could tell. I know what you're saying: "Fruit flies?" And I'll answer you: "Yes! FRUIT FLIES!"

I told you that I politely tried to usher them out. I escorted them out! I didn't even raise my voice. I was kind! But they were just . . . there . . . constantly! And then one day it got too much and I swatted! I mean, with my hand! And it was not so much a swat as a wave, a gentle wave. Only I guess I . . . I looked at my hand and I had . . . got one. It was an accident! But you can't tell them that. No! I quickly went to the sink to wash my hands, but they knew.

And from that day forward things changed. They weren't on the periphery any more, settling on an unfinished glass of wine or coffee or dishes or the trash. I would walk into my kitchen and my white cabinets would be literally covered with black flecks. It was . . . an invasion! I couldn't help myself, they were camped in specific areas, and I would slap at them, sometimes squishing them against the painted woodwork. They would simply move to another area. To the walls, or the appliances. Then I developed a strategy. I would spray them with water from a little . . . spritzer thing. This wouldn't really hurt them, I told myself. But then I began spritzing them, and they would get the water stuck in their wings, making them easy targets. I would take out dozens at once. One day I reached for the Windex, and I sprayed and killed and cleaned at the same time.

I can't even tell you what was happening to me, but it became like a mission. The thorough annihilation of these . . . I began keeping a tally. I set up traps, just a bit of sticky jam on a knife, or a drop of honey on the countertop, and I would wait until a group of them had gathered and then WHAM, leaving the carcasses in place as a warning to others. They tried to retreat, to the living room and bedroom, but I was always one step ahead of them.

And at one point I noticed it . . . when I would kill them, press them against a hard surface until they crumpled under

the pressure . . . when I would wipe the pieces of body away
. . . there was blood.
    Fruit flies. Right.

Two Girls

ERIN CRESSIDA WILSON

A forty-year-old woman remembers falling in love with a woman in college.

She had slits of blue eyes, and cigarettes popping in and out of her mouth. Like cherry coke around her lips, she looked like she had just sipped something and not wiped her mouth—very red lips that were thin and a little cruel. Black mascara and blonde hair like feathers just above her scalp. She was a punk rocker from East Cambridge, with the voice of Jody Foster, black leather leg warmers, and a camera that she held onto for dear life—nighttime flash photography of dismal places. I had met her in my Advanced Nude Photography Seminar. She showed me pictures of burned down houses and I imagined making love to her inside of them. She showed me altars to her boyfriend and I imagined knocking them down. Her room was like the child's room I had always wanted. I convinced her to get into my dorm by telling her to go cry to the Dean, and the next thing I knew she not only lived with me and one hundred other women, but she was my best friend, and we smoked on her single bed as the snow fell on my birthday, and she took me out into the cold, gave me a rocking horse and a bottle of champagne, and thoroughly made me fall in love with her as we passed by the swing that Martha swung on in the movie version of *Who's Afraid of Virginia Woolf.* It was not until after we graduated that one night we found ourselves in an 80s hot tub, all by ourselves, after all the loser older Townies left, and she asked if she could kiss me—oh God—and she leapt across the water at me and took my face in her hands, and for the first time I felt a woman kissing me—and George Winston was playing—and I smelled cedar and chemicals or whatever hot tubs are made of, and she was climbing all over me, slipping across my white body with her tiny nipples, and she told me how beautiful I was. And later, inside the shower, she looked at me like the end of the world as I closed my eyes and imagined the burned out house she would make love to me in, and how I would not run away from this promised life—love of women and every single fucking thing that goes along with it, but I would stay with the dyke in me, embrace the fucking amazon, open up my chest to the world that would spit upon me, and run away with her forever, this girl that I had fallen in love with the second I caught a glimpse of her slit blue eyes. But I didn't. I turned away. I never inserted a finger inside another woman or really even inside myself. I'd say, "I don't do that with women, go below the belt, the taste, no." So I went through my twenties with semen shot down my throat, and I swallowed every time, wondering about everything I had missed the moment Elena plunged her fingers inside me—my best friend—and I started to cry, and I said, "No" as I grabbed my clothes and ran from the room. In 1985. At Smith College.

Breathing Space

BETTY JANE WYLIE

FLORRIE, an old woman, is lying in her bed in a small bedroom in a private house. The lighting is dim and comes from odd sources: moonlight (or a street lamp?) falling through the window; a thin strip of light under the door leading to the rest of the house; a red glow from her heating pad switch; the white clock light on her VCR; the red digital lights of the numbers on her clock radio by the bed. She is awake and restless, tossing and turning, but not vigorously. She's probably in some pain but she's not a complainer, even to herself.

FLORRIE: This pillow is so lovely and soft you could be on a cloud. (*Pause*) Perhaps that's what it's like up there, out there—wherever—like a plump cloud, like a lofty pillow. Aloft! Be terrible if you were allergic to feathers. That's all right, now there's polyester. You wander lonely as a cloud, stuffed full of polyester.

You like that white light on the video box? (*She sits up.*) If you get close enough you can see the time but even the glow is pleasant from the bed and keeps the dark away. Then there's the little red light when the heating pad's on, that's comforting too. Best of all is the time light on your bed table, right here all the time, red numbers telling you the time in the night. (*She examines the clock.*) 3:26 a.m. Three little lights tell you you're still alive. Clock, video, heater. What more do you need? Maybe that's all there is.

Yesterday—was it yesterday? Maybe. Yesterday or some time lately you noticed that the time on the video is different from the time by your bed. It was three or four minutes' difference, which is quite a lot when you come to think of it.

Now that you've thought of it, you'd like to know, wouldn't you? Like to know exactly how big the difference is. What would it cost?

Leaving this warm bed for one. (*She throws the covers off and with some difficulty swings her feet out of the bed.*) Getting your feet cold for two—yes, both of them. You won't need slippers though, you're coming right back. Glasses? No, if you get close enough, you can see the numbers without your glasses. (*She stands up and shuffles over to the television set, bends to examine the numbers, talking all the while.*) Little white numbers clicking your life away. Catch them in the act. 3:23 (*She shuffles back, still talking.*) Twenty-three minutes after three in the morning. Doesn't feel like morning. Too dark for morning. Feels like the middle of the night. Over there—here—now . . . (*She reads the numbers on her digital clock.*) 3:27 Twenty-seven minutes after three, the same morning.

So—there's a whole four minutes between the wall and the bed, that is, between the video box and the radio clock. Four minutes extra breathing time for you. Anything could happen in four minutes. You could relive that time. What would you rather do? While you still can. Maybe. Four extra minutes of light, or darkness—air, anyway. Breathing time.

Maybe you are being incautious. Maybe you shouldn't let on you know about those extra minutes. Never know when they will come in handy. Don't tell. Someone knows, though. Someone out there knows, out there beyond your mind, outside this room where they decide whether you live or whether you die, out there, somewhere. Maybe you shouldn't let on. They don't like sharing secrets. They know you're still here. You aren't telling them anything they don't know, that you're still warm and glowing, like a little light in the night. (*She has climbed into bed again and is trying to get warm.*) Glowing? You wouldn't go as far as to say that. Warm? Fairly warm. Your feet will be fine in a minute, just push the heating pad against them. . . . There. Cozy. Almost. Not very. Not very warm. You always did have cold hands and feet. Edward used to tell you not to come to bed until your feet were warm. How could your feet get warm without his back to warm them on? It is not good for man to be alone, no, nor woman neither, for how can one be warm in bed? How else will she warm her feet?

Hence the heating pad. Hence? Don't ever say hence to them. Not even Andrew. People say you live with them, with Andrew and Isabel, but that's not true. Truth is they live with you. You wouldn't leave this house. How could you ever leave this house? Edward carried you into this house sixty-eight years ago. Someone else will carry you out. Still a good house. Big. Lots of rooms. Isabel likes it too, you can tell, but she'll never let on to you.

Isabel—what is her last name? Now, if she used your name, Edward's name, Andrew's name, Jason's name, Ellie's name, you'd know, you wouldn't have this problem. There's three sounds to it. Munch kin son. Like that but not that. Hen der son. No. Al bert son. Maybe not son. Maybe ton. Ed mon ton. No no. Stupid. What do you want to know for, anyway? What's it to you? That's what Jason says. "What's it to you?" "Don't get smart with your grandmother," she says when he talks like that. What's he to Hecuba or Hecuba to him? What's it to you? "Who's Hecuba?" You can hear her asking if you ever said that out loud. For Heaven's sake, don't ever say anything like that out loud. She would look at you as if you were dotty, no idea of what you were talking about. That's how she looks at you most of the time. She looks at you as if you have finally lost all your marbles. Not finally. Not yet. There's more where those came from, and she has more of those looks too. She has lots of looks. She is a good woman. She just fusses too much. Fuss er ton. That's it! Fesserton, that's her name. You knew you could do it if you tried. Aren't you glad that's settled?

Fesserton. It should be Fusserton. She certainly does fuss a lot. You used to do that—fuss. Sometimes it seemed like you spent your whole life fussing. Well, if women didn't fuss, who would? You don't fuss any more, hardly ever. Everything you fussed about either happened or it didn't. Mostly it went away. So don't complain. You have nothing to complain about. Count your blessings.

You think they like living with you? Yes. Most of the time, yes, they do. You don't bother them much, hardly know you're here. You heard her say that on the phone. "She's so quiet most of the time, we hardly know she's here." Sometimes you have to look at yourself to see if you still are . . . yup, still here. "She's really no trouble." Doesn't bother them as much as it does you, being like this, halfway between there and here. You really are. Halfway between. Four minutes between, anyway. Four minutes between here and there, then and now. Anything could happen.

This is not using your four minutes well, blathering away like this. Four minutes between the wall and the bed and all you can do is blather. Use the time well. That's what your father used to say. And Mrs. Bynge, remember her? How can you come up with Mrs. Bynge's name and you take a year and a half to remember your own daughter-in-law's maiden name that she still uses even though she's not a maiden any more, not with Ellie and Jason here to prove it, she's not. Isabel Fesserton, see? You remembered. So you can remember Mrs. Bynge if you want to.

Where were you? What were you saying—thinking? Yes, yes, about time and using it well, and Mrs. Bynge used to say, "Let me not lose its moments." That was for your first pregnancy—for Andrew. You told her you were expecting a baby and she said the best blessing she could wish you was consciousness. Cherish the moments.

And now, here, you've been given four extra moments of consciousness. Time past and time present, four minutes earlier over there than it is here and you're caught in the middle, halfway between the past and the future. Was ever woman so blessed? What are you going to do about it? Don't you lose those moments, Flo honey. Hang on to them. As Andrew would say, hang in there, Florrie. Starting now.

It's 3:29 already. Oh dear. But over there it's only 3:25, so you're all right. One Mississippi two Mississippi three Mississippi.

Get back to the subject at hand: four minutes to change the world. Given the right four minutes, you could, you really could, solve the problems of the world. Given the fulcrum you could lift the world. "What's a fulcrum?" she'll say. Would Jason know what a fulcrum is? Ask him sometime. How would you bring it up? Hard to bring up fulcrums in an ordinary conversation. Please pass the salt. Where do you put the fulcrum to move the world?

That was the whole picture, wasn't it? There was never a place to stand. "Listen to her. She's getting dotty." You are not! You are not as dotty or as simple as you look. Nothing is.

Actually, everything is. Even simpler, in fact. Dead simple.

"What is the secret of life?" she'll say. No, she'd never say that. Nor would Andrew. Jason, maybe, when he's older. But Ellie, now, Ellie might say it now. She'll look at you as the world turns and say, "What is the secret of life, Grandma?" Then you'll say, what will you say? You'll say, four minutes, Ellie. Four minutes of pure love. If everyone loved everyone else for four whole minutes without stopping, why the world would turn, would truly turn on its axis.

Then you wouldn't need a fulcrum.

Why didn't anyone ever tell you that before?

Maybe they did and you weren't listening. They told you now—no, they didn't. You figured it out all by yourself. Because you had the time. You had four extra minutes of uncounted time to figure it out. Four minutes and a place to stand and you can change the world.

Why didn't anyone ever figure that out before?

You're losing it now. It's running out.

Not if you know it's there. Not if you reach and touch and hold it, let it slip deliciously through your gnarled old fingers and count it like daisy petals.

Cherish the moments.

Will you remember this in the morning? Will you even be here in the morning?

No.

You know that, don't you? You were given four extra minutes to be calm, sort yourself out, count your blessings, breathe quietly. (*She lies down, settles herself under the blanket and sighs.*)

Yes, yes.

So be properly grateful. You are. (*Getting very sleepy.*)

You are grateful, always have been.

You should thank the Management, or someone.

It was quite nice while it lasted.

Contributors

Joan Ackermann is cofounder and artistic director of Mixed Company in Great Barrington, Massachusetts, a year-round theatre now in its twenty-second year. Her plays include *Zara Spook and Other Lures* (1990 Humana Festival), *Stanton's Garage* (1993 Humana Festival), *The Batting Cage* (1999 Humana Festival), *Don't Ride the Clutch*, *Bed and Breakfast*, *Rescuing Greenland*, *Isabella*, *A Knight at the Theatre*, *Back Story*, and *Off the Map*. She adapted *Off the Map* into a screenplay, and the film will be released in 2004. Her plays have been produced at The Vineyard Theatre in New York, Circle Rep, The George Street Theatre, Cleveland Play House, Shakespeare & Company, The Berkshire Theatre Festival, Mark Taper Forum, and The Atlantic Theatre Company. She has also written and produced for television.

Liz Duffy Adams is a member of New Dramatists. Her plays, which include *Dog Act*, *The Train Play*, and *A Wrinkle in Time*, have been produced or developed at Bay Area Playwrights Festival, Portland Center Stage, Syracuse Stage, and Women's Project & Productions, among other places. Anthologized works include *Poodle with Guitar and Dark Glasses* in *Best American Short Plays 2000–2001* (Applause Books). "Cantaloupe" was commissioned by Joanne Jacobson for the New Dramatists Writers Benefit 2002.

Janet Allard is a recipient of two Jerome Fellowships at The Playwrights' Center (2000–2001, 2002–2003). Her recent works include *Incognito* (commissioned by the Guthrie Theater) and *Loyal* (a joint commission of the Guthrie and The Children's Theatre Company in Minneapolis). *The Unknown: a silent musical* (a collaboration with director Jean Randich and composer Shane Rettig) was awarded a Jonathan Larson Fellowship and received a concert/reading at MTC in 2003. *The Untold Crimes of Insomniacs* premiered at the Guthrie Theater in 2004. Allard's work has been seen at The Kennedy Center, Playwrights Horizons, Yale Rep, The Yale Cabaret, The Women's Project & Productions, The House of Candles, Access Theatre, and in Ireland, England, Greece, and New Zealand.

Rachel Axler's plays have been produced by Vital Theatre Company, Spring Theatreworks, Cal Arts, and other companies in the New York and Los Angeles regions. Her work can be read at mcsweeneys.com and in various bathroom stalls across the United States. She received her B.A. from Williams College and her M.F.A. in playwriting from UCSD.

Bianca Bagatourian received her B.F.A. from the Art Center College of Design in Pasadena, California, and spent fifteen years making commercials, videos, and television shows. *The Scent of Jasmine* (from which "The Strawberry Scene" is taken) is her first full-length play. Her one-act *Men* was produced in an Off-Off-Broadway Festival in 2003. *Giraffe*, another short play, was produced as part of the TSI/Playtime Series in New York in 2003. She is currently working on *Baku '89*, a story of the atrocities committed in the Caucasus region, which she came across while doing interviews on a recent visit there.

Neena Beber's plays include *Jump/Cut* (premiered at Woolly Mammoth/Theatre J), *Hard Feelings* (The Women's Project & Productions), *A Common Vision* (The Magic Theatre), *Tomorrowland* (New Georges), *The Brief but Exemplary Life of the Living Goddess* (The Magic), and *Failure to Thrive* (Padua Hills Playwrights Festival). Beber has been a recipient of the ASK Exchange to The Royal Court Theatre, the L. Arnold Weissberger Award for Playwriting, a MacDowell Colony Fellowship, grants from AT&T and the NEA, and commissions from Playwrights Horizons and Otterbein College. Many of her one-acts were first presented at HB Playwrights Foundation, where *A Body of Water* premiered. Beber is a member of New Dramatists.

Brooke Berman's work has been produced at Steppenwolf Theatre Company, The Play Company, The Second Stage, the Humana Festival, The Round Table Ensemble, and Naked Angels. She has received a Berilla Kerr award, a Helen Merrill award, two Francesca Primus awards, and a Lila Acheson Wallace American Playwrights Fellowship. Berman is the Playwright Mentor to the MCC Youth Company, where she teaches playwriting to New York City public high school students. Originally a solo performer, she is now a member of New Dramatists, Rising Phoenix Rep, and the Dramatists Guild. "Winter with Tambourine Boy" is from *The Liddy Plays*.

Meredith Besser is a fiction writer, personal essayist, editor, and journalist living in sunny Southern California, after living in New York, Japan, and Bulgaria. She has been published in the *Los Angeles Times*, writes a quirky column for a local newsletter, and is working on her first full-length play.

Deborah Brevoort is the author of numerous plays and musicals, including *The Women of Lockerbie* (Onassis International Playwriting Competition), *Signs of Life* (Jane Chambers Award), *Into the Fire* (Weissberger Award) and *The Poetry of Pizza*. She is a two-time winner of the Frederick Lowe Award in Musical Theatre, first for *King Island Christmas*, with composer David Friedman, and later for *Coyote Goes Salmon Fishing*, with composer Scott Richards. She is an alumnus of New Dramatists.

Sharon Bridgforth wrote *con flama* as a National Endowment for the Arts/Theatre Communications Group Playwright in Residence at Frontera@Hyde Park Theatre. *con flama* received the Rockefeller Foundation Multi-Arts Production Fund Award in support of the collaboration between Bridgforth (playwright), Laurie Carlos (director), and Lourdes Perez (composer), and was produced as a 2002 mainstage show at Penumbra Theatre Company in St. Paul, Minnesota.

Kim Brundidge currently lives in the Atlanta area. Her work has been performed at Push Push Theater, 7 Stages, Actor's Express, and Clark Atlanta University; it has been workshopped at Theatre in the Square and Horizon Theater, and has won awards at the Georgia Theatre Conference and the University of Louisville Juneteenth Festival. Brundidge is a member of the Dramatists Guild and on the staff at Alliance Theatre as a teaching artist. "I Am Not a Black Woman" is taken from her play *Past Eve: A Meditation on Mothers and Sons.*

Sheila Callaghan's plays have been produced and developed with ASK Theatre Projects, Playwrights Horizons, South Coast Repertory, Actors Theatre of Louisville, New Georges, Annex Theatre, and LABrynth, among others. She is the winner of the 2000 Princess Grace award, as well as the recipient of a MacDowell Fellowship and a Jerome Fellowship. Her plays include *Scab, Kate Crackernuts, The Hunger Waltz, The Catherine Calamity, Dead City,* and *Crawl Fade to White.* Among her current projects are commissions from EST/Sloan and South Coast Repertory, a postmodern adaptation of Joyce's *Ulysses,* and a modern opera entitled *Elemental,* with composer Sophocles Papavasilopoulos.

Darrah Cloud's plays include *The House Across the Street, The Stick Wife,* an adaptation of *O Pioneers!* (with Kim D. Sherman), the stage adaptation of Jose Donoso's *The Obscene Bird of Night, The Sirens, Dream House, The Boxcar Children, The Braille Garden, American Siddhartha, Honor Song for Crazy Horse* and *Heartland* (both with Kim D. Sherman), a commission for the Clear Channel entitled *Makeover!,* the lyrics for the musical adaptation of Willy Holtzman's play, *Sabina,* and an adaptation of *Snow White* for Disneyland. Her awards include grants from the NEA and the Rockefeller Foundation, the Frederick Loewe Musical Theatre Award, the Roger L. Stevens Award, and a Gilman and Gonzalez-Falla Musical Theatre Commendation Award.

Constance Congdon's *Tales of the Lost Formicans* has had over 150 productions worldwide. *Dog Opera* and *Casanova* premiered at the New York Shakespeare Festival; *Lips* premiered at Primary Stages in New York City. Other plays include *Losing Father's Body, No Mercy, One Day Earlier, Native American, Dark Bridge Mountain, Gilgamesh, Phantomnation* (with Mac Wellman), and *So Far.* Congdon has also written librettos for four operas, the most recent one, *Earthrise* (for Pulitzer Prize–winning composer Lewis Spratlan) is scheduled for production by the San Francisco Opera in 2004. Congdon's newest play, *A Mother,* will be produced at ACT. Congdon currently teaches playwriting at Amherst College and the Yale School of Drama.

Tönya Derrickson grew up in Talkeetna, Alaska, received a degree in theater, and drove to Seattle, Washington. She has worked as an actor and director but enjoys most the craft of writing. Her plays include *A Question of Wills, the AnNe WaR, Anthem of Master Ed,* and *The Asshole Dance.* Tönya also writes poetry and has performed her work in Los Angeles, Seattle, and New York.

Constance Dial was a member of the Los Angeles Police Department for nearly 27 years. In 1999, she retired as a captain and the commanding officer of the Hollywood Division. Prior to her police career, she was a journalist and photographer and is now a full-time writer of plays, novels, and short stories.

Donna DiNovelli is a playwright and librettist whose work has been performed at the New York City Opera, Joseph Papp Public Theater, Mark Taper Forum, and Joe's Pub. She has been commissioned by BBC radio, Chanticleer (the Grammy Award–winning singing group), and the Manhattan Theater Club. She has been a Resident Artist at Mabou Mines and has taught at Brown University, NYU/Tisch School of the Arts, and the National Theater Institute.

Linda Eisenstein is a three-time recipient of Ohio Arts Council Individual Artist Playwriting Fellowships for *Three the Hard Way* and the musicals *Star Wares: The Next Generation* and *Discordia* (with James Levin). Other plays include *The Names of the Beast* (Sappho's Symposium Award) and *Marla's Devotion* (All-England Festival Prize). Her works have been produced throughout the U.S. and abroad. She is a member of the Cleveland Play House Playwrights' Unit.

Annie Evans' *Ghost Stories* has been produced around the world. Her other plays have been produced at Actors Theatre of Louisville, Manhattan Class Company, New York Stage and Film Company, Circle Repertory Company, Circle East, New Georges, The Ensemble Studio Theatre, The Asolo Theatre Center, The Hudson Theatre, The Westbank Cafe, and The Eugene O'Neill National Playwrights Conference, among others. Her monologues "I Can't Stop Thinking Today" and "Breasts" are published in anthologies by Heinemann Books. "Breasts" was also performed on WPLR. She's written for PBS, Disney Channel, Nickelodeon, Animal Planet and the Cartoon Network. She currently writes for *Sesame Street* (five Emmy awards).

Nell Grantham is the alter ego of a librarian who hails from the rectangular states of the Midwest but currently lives in Virginia. Thanks and big love to the No Shame family (www.noshame.org) for turning this audience member into a writer and performer. Look for other works by this author at www.ristentltd.com.

Rinne Groff is a playwright and performer, a founding member of Elevator Repair Service experimental theater company, and an instructor in NYU's Department of Dramatic Writing. Her plays include *Orange Lemon Egg Canary, Jimmy Carter Was a Democrat, Inky, The Five Hysterical Girls Theorem,* and *The Ruby Sunrise.* She is a member of the Dramatists Guild, a Usual Suspect at New York Theatre Workshop, and an associate of Target Margin and Clubbed Thumb theaters. She graduated from Yale in 1991 and NYU in 1999.

Ellen Hagan is a writer, performer, and educator. She holds an M.F.A. in fiction from The New School and has received grants from the Kentucky Foundation for Women. She has self-published several chapbooks, and her work can be seen in the online journals *La Petite Zine* and *Failbetter.* She is currently working on her first novel, *The Kentucky Notes.*

Imani Harrington's writings include plays, book reviews, poetry, editorials, and interviews. She is coeditor of *Positive/Negative: Women of*

Color and HIV/AIDS, an anthology of plays, prose, and poetry (Aunt Lute, 2002). Harrington is the winner of the Bay Area Poets and Writers Award for fiction, the Giorno Poetry Award, a Culture Equity Grant to Individual Artists, and a recipient of Serpent Source funding as well as the PEN American West grant. Her plays are *Love & Danger, Do You Have the Time to Die?, En El Jardin, Master Swimmer, In Seven Moons*, and a fangled animal hip hopera, *Dog, Frog, Bear, Flea and Queen Bee*.

Jean Kristen Hedgecock earned her B.A. from UNC at Chapel Hill and her M.A. from Columbia University. Her plays have been performed in New York at The Pulse Ensemble Theatre and the Lion Theatre as well as at The Orpheum, The William Inge Theatre Festival, The Edward Albee Last Frontier Festival, the Mid-America Theatre Conference, the Boston Playwrights' Theatre, and others. She is a writer-in-residence and member of the advisory board for Streetlight Productions in New York.

Elizabeth Heffron's plays include *Mitzi's Abortion* (commissioned by ACT Theatre for the FringeACT Festival of New Plays) and *New Patagonia* (produced by the Seattle Repertory Theatre). Her work has been staged in Seattle, Vancouver B.C., New York, St. Louis, and San Francisco. She's the recipient of three Seattle Artist grants from the Seattle Arts Commission, and a Playwriting Fellowship from Artist Trust and the Washington State Arts Commission.

Lindsay Brandon Hunter is an actor and playwright living in New York City. Her plays include *Licking Spalding Gray* (cowritten with Ben Laurance), *Like this*, and *Que Sera, My Darling*. Her work has been performed at On the Boards' 12 Minutes Max series and at Seattle's Mae West Fest and 14/48 festivals.

Carleen Jaspers has recently returned to her birthplace, the Glacial Lakes region of northeastern South Dakota. She teaches Fine Arts and Spanish at Roslyn School, a K–12 institution of 150 students. Carleen is a member of the Dramatists Guild of America. "Anymore" is excerpted from her full-length play, *Impurities*, which was developed at both Play Works and WordBRIDGE script-tanks.

Susan Johnston received her M.F.A. from NYU's Tisch School of the Arts and was a 2002/03 Jerome Fellow at The Playwrights' Center of Minneapolis. Her plays for teens, *Death of the Smiley Face* and *Lizzie Loves Joe Loves Sharon*, are available through Eldridge Publishing. Recent productions include *Old Woman Flying* at Mill Mountain Theatre and *One Girl Drummer,* commissioned and produced by City Lights Youth Theatre. She also writes for *Interview Magazine* and A&E's *Biography.*

Honour Kane's plays have been produced by the Public Theatre New Works, Sydney's Annual Mardi Gras Arts Festival, New Georges, Actors Theatre of Louisville, BACA Downtown, The Theatre Outlet in Allentown, Pennsylvania, and Ireland's Inishbofin Arts Festival. A current New Dramatist, she is the past recipient of a National Endowment for the Arts Playwriting Fellowship, a Bunting Fellowship at Harvard/Radcliffe, a Pew Fellowship in the Arts, as well as MacDowell and Yaddo residencies.

Aurorae Khoo held a 2001–2002 Bunting Fellowship in playwriting at Harvard/Radcliffe, where she wrote *HappyValley.* She also wrote for the CBS television action-drama *Walker, Texas Ranger.* Her play *The Double Auntie Waltz* won the Kennedy Center's Edgar L. Stevens Award in 2000. Khoo earned an M.F.A. from New York University and a B.A. in East Asian Studies from Brown University. She currently teaches undergraduate screenwriting at the University of Southern California.

Marty Kingsbury received her M.F.A. in playwriting from Brandeis University in 1993. Her work has been produced in her hometown Boston area as well as in Cleveland, New York City, Atlanta, and Eugene, Oregon. Internationally it has also been seen in London and Sydney. Her one-act play, *Scent of Tulips,* was published in *Tough Acts to Follow* (Alamo Square). "And What She Told Me" comes from her play *Lucille.*

Lisa M. Konoplisky is a playwright, director, and actor living in Madison, Wisconsin, and currently completing her M.F.A. in playwriting at Columbia College in Chicago, where she also taught for several years. Lisa worked with Theatre X and American Inside Theatre in Milwaukee as well as the University Theatre in Madison. Her plays have been produced in New York, Chicago, and Edinburgh, Scotland. She is a two-time winner of the Vitality Playwriting Contest at Speaking Ring Theater in Chicago and her play *White Elephant* will have a staged reading at The Stockyards Theatre Project in Chicago in 2004. She teaches acting and playwriting for children at Children's Theatre of Madison and Madison Community Arts Program.

Sherry Kramer's work has been seen at theaters across America and abroad. She is a recipient of NEA, New York Foundation for the Arts, and McKnight Fellowships, the Weissberger Playwriting Award, a New York Drama League Award, and the Marvin Taylor Award (for *What A Man Weighs*), the LA Women in Theater New Play Award (for *The Wall of Water*), and the Jane Chambers Playwriting Award (for *David's RedHaired Death*). The first national member of New Dramatists, she teaches playwriting at the Michener Center for Writers at the University of Texas, Austin, and at the Iowa Playwrights Workshop. Her plays are published by Broadway Publishing. "Diet Cherry Coke" is excerpted from *The Mad Master*.

Mary Lathrop's plays, which include *The Visible Horse, Dreams of Baby, Menstruating Waitress from Hell*, and *The Six Basic Rules*, have been developed at the National Playwrights Conference, the Ojai Playwrights Conference, and Seven Devils Playwrights Conference and produced by theatres in Seattle, New York, Chicago, Los Angeles, Dallas, and elsewhere. Awards include the Richard Hugo House New Play Prize and the Mill Mountain Theatre New Play Competition. *The Urn of Drew* was a finalist for the Susan Smith Blackburn Prize and *Tales from the Saltmines* received Honorable Mention from the Jane Chambers Playwriting Contest. She has received fellowships in playwriting from the Washington State Arts Commission, the Seattle Arts Commission, and Artist Trust. She teaches playwriting at the University of Washington.

Michele Lowe made her Broadway debut with *The Smell of the Kill*, which has productions scheduled for theatres throughout the U.S. and in Canada, Greece, Germany, and Switzerland. *String of Pearls* premiered at City Theatre in Pittsburgh, and *Backsliding in the Promised Land* premiered at Syracuse Stage. *Map of Heaven* was featured in the ASK New Play Weekend and at the Syracuse Stage New Play Festival. Lowe wrote the book and lyrics for *Hit the Lights!*, a musical chosen for the National Music Center Theater Conference. Her work has been produced at the Intiman Theatre, Berkshire Theater Festival, The Vineyard Theatre, the Delaware Theatre Company, Reykjavik City Theatre (Iceland), Round House Theatre, Capital Rep, Cleveland Play House, and Cincinnati Playhouse in the Park.

Ellen McLaughlin's productions include *The Persians* (National Actors' Theater), *A Narrow Bed* (New York Theater Workshop and Actors Theatre of Louisville), *Tongue of a Bird* and *Helen* (both at The Public Theater), *Iphigenia and Other Daughters* (Classic Stage Company, New York), and *Days and Nights Within* and *Infinity's House* (both at Actors

Theatre of Louisville). Other producing venues include The Mark Taper Forum, The Intiman Theater, Oregon Shakespeare Festival, and The Almeida Theater in London. She has received NEA awards, the Susan Smith Blackburn Prize, and awards from the Lila Wallace–Reader's Digest Fund.

Ana Maria Mebane is a writer/actor who is just starting out her life in Los Angeles after finishing up school at Emerson College in Boston, Massachusetts. The piece in this volume is from her one-woman show entitled *She Always Told Me: On the Socialization of American Females*.

Susan Mendelsohn is a playwright and dramaturg. Her plays have been produced in New York, London, Seattle, and New Haven. Two plays, *Domestic Chaos* and *Eaglestones*, examine women's health issues within the historical medical paradigm. New play dramaturgy credits include Sundance Playwrights Lab, New York Stage and Film, Voice and Visions, and the Gertrude Stein Repertory Company. She holds an M.F.A. from the Yale School of Drama.

S. P. Miskowski interned with New City Theater in 1992. The following year she was awarded a National Endowment for the Arts Fellowship and an M.F.A. Since then, her work has been recognized with readings, commissions, workshops, and productions at A Contemporary Theatre, Asylum, Cherry Lane Alternative, City3 Theater, GEVA, and the University of Washington. She appears in three Smith & Kraus anthologies; four of her plays are published by Rain City Projects.

Stephanie Moore's work has been cited in *New York Stories Notable Stories* 2002. She was a Pushcart Prize Nominee, a Marin Arts Council Fiction Grant winner, and a Writer's Digest Short Story winner. She currently serves as the director of the Writer's Workshop in Mill Valley. Her stories have been published extensively in the United States and Canada.

Julie Marie Myatt has been produced in New York, Los Angeles, San Francisco, Minneapolis, and Actors Theatre of Louisville. Her plays include *August is a thin girl, The Sex Habits of American Women, The Pink Factor, Cowbird, Alice in the Badlands, Clamor,* and *49 Days to the Sun. Zealot* and *The Joy of Having a Body* were commissioned by the Guthrie Theater. Her other published plays include *Lift and Bang* and *What he sent.* Myatt received a Walt Disney Studios Screenwriting Fellowship in 1992–1993, a Jerome Fellowship at the Playwrights' Center in

1999–2000, and a McKnight Advancement Grant for 2001–2002, and is a participant in the Guthrie Theater New Play Project.

Jamie Pachino's plays *Waving Goodbye, The Return to Morality, Aurora's Motive,* and *Race* have won over a dozen awards, including the Kennedy Center Fund for New American Plays and Chicago's Joseph Jefferson ("Jeff") Award for Best New Work. Her work has been seen in four countries, and commissioned, published, and optioned for the screen. She is currently at work on a new play commission for Steppenwolf Theatre and screenplays for DreamWorks, Walden Media, and Lifetime television.

Regina Porter is a graduate of New York University's Tisch School of the Arts. Her plays have been produced regionally and in New York. She has been commissioned by The Public Theater, The Women's Project & Productions, Actors Theatre of Louisville, and Playwrights Horizons. She lives in Brooklyn, New York, with her husband and daughter.

Susanna Ralli is a playwright and editor in the Boston area. Her short plays, which include *An Allergic Reaction, Critique, When the Dead Woman Speaks,* and *Instant Karma,* have been produced in Boston, Rhode Island, New York, and Greece. Her monologue "The Road" was published in *Even More Monologues for Women by Women.* She is a member of the Dramatists Guild.

Jacquelyn Reingold's plays, which include *String Fever, Girl Gone, Dear Kenneth Blake, Tunnel of Love, Freeze Tag, Acapulco,* and *For-everett,* have been seen in New York at Ensemble Studio Theatre, MCC, Naked Angels, and HB Playwrights. She has been the recipient of the New Dramatists' Whitfield Cook and Joe Callaway awards, two Drama-Logues, and funding through an EST/Sloan Commission and the Kennedy Center's Fund for New American Plays. She expects to receive her M.F.A. in playwriting in 2004 from Ohio University.

Tania Richard's plays include *Happy. Go. Lucky* (finalist, Seanachi Theatre's Amarach Play Festival), *Selecting Memory* (winner, Seanachi Theatre's Amarach Play Festival), *Variations on a Theme* (finalist, Famous Doors—Women at the Door), *Tru Imagined Life* (Equity Library Theatre's Outreach), *Bitty Danvers' Family Stump, An Evening with Renee Lawrence,* and *Internally Yours.* She was commissioned by Healthworks Theatre to write an original script on HIV prevention. She holds a B.S. in Theatre from Illinois State University.

Kate Robin's plays include *Anon, Intrigue With Faye, The Light Outside, Swimming in March* (winner of the IRNE Best Play of 2001 award), *Bride Stripped Bare, Given Away,* and *Stigmata & Other Symptoms.* Her awards and honors are a Princess Grace Fellowship, a Whitfield Cook Award, serving as a Brooks Atkinson Exchange Playwright to the Royal National Theatre, and the 2003 Princess Grace Statue Award. Robin is an alumna of New Dramatists. Currently, she is writing an original screenplay for Working Title and is a Writer/Producer on HBO's drama *Six Feet Under.*

Sarah Ruhl's plays include *The Clean House, Melancholy Play, Eurydice, Late: a cowboy song, Orlando,* and *Passion Play.* Her plays have been produced in New York, London, Chicago, Los Angeles, Louisville, Minneapolis, Madison, and Providence. Originally from Chicago, she received her M.F.A. from Brown University. In 2003, she was the recipient of a Helen Merrill award and a Whiting Writers' award.

Buffy Sedlachek is a resident artist with Stages Theatre Company, literary manager of The Jungle Theater, associate director of the Guthrie Theater's Schools on Stage, and a core alum of The Playwrights' Center. A five-time Playlabs writer, nominated three times for The Susan Smith Blackburn Prize, she received three McKnight Advancement Grants, two Jones Fellowships, two Minnesota State Arts Board Fellowships, a TCG observatorship, and a Jerome Travel and Study Grant, among others. *Under Yelena* played at InterAct Theatre in Philadelphia and at The Cricket Theatre in Minneapolis.

Betty Shamieh is a Palestinian-American playwright and actress. She performed her play of monologues *Chocolate in Heat,* which sold out at the 2001 New York International Fringe Festival and has subsequently been presented at over fifteen venues across the country. Her play *Roar* was presented Off-Broadway at the New Group. A graduate of Harvard University and the Yale School of Drama, she received the 2001 New Dramatists Van Lier Fellowship. She is the screenwriting professor at Marymount Manhattan College.

Jane Shepard's works have been produced around the country and received multiple accolades, including the Berrilla Kerr Playwriting Award, a New York Foundation for the Arts Fellowship, a Sloan Foundation Science grant, and a Writer's Guild nomination for Best Screenplay for her Showtime original movie *Freak City.* She wishes to acknowledge director Julie Hamberg and actress Donna Jean Fogel for their contributions to the original production of *God Is A Dyke*.

Lillian Ann Slugocki is an award-winning novelist, playwright, and producer and a regular contributor for Salon.com. She created, produced, and co-authored the critically acclaimed *The Erotica Project*, with Erin Cressida Wilson, produced Off-Broadway and published by Cleis Press. She contributed a one-act play, *2001: An Oral History*, for Brave New World's commemoration of September 11th produced on Broadway and has just completed a full-length erotic novel, *Diary of a Divorce*.

Caridad Svich is resident playwright at New Dramatists. Her plays have been produced across the U.S. and abroad at venues as diverse as 7 Stages, Salvage Vanguard Theatre, Cincinnati Playhouse, and the Traverse Theatre. Her translations are collected in *Federico Garcia Lorca: Impossible Theater* (Smith & Kraus). She holds an M.F.A. from UCSD and is on the advisory committee of *Contemporary Theatre Review*. Awards include grants from TCG, NEA, and a Bunting Fellowship from Harvard/Radcliffe.

C. Denby Swanson is a graduate of Smith College, the National Theatre Institute, and the University of Texas Michener Center for Writers, where she was a Michener Fellow in Playwriting and Screenwriting. She has been produced by Salvage Vanguard Theatre, 15 Head, The Drilling Company, and others, and is published by Playscripts, Inc. She has been a William Inge Playwright in Residence, a Jerome Fellow, and a McKnight Advancement Grant recipient. She currently resides in the New York area.

Fiona J. Torres' work has been published by Broadway Play Publishing, *The Amherst Review, The South Carolina Review,* and *Diaolgue*. It has been performed at South Coast Rep, ACT/Hedgebrook Women Playwrights Festival, Brava!, Live Girls!, Cornish College, Seattle Opera, Opera Idaho, La Casa de Artes, and on various radio venues.

Jennie Webb is an LA-based playwright whose works staged at theatres across the country include *Remodeling Plans, The Complete Story of the War* (The Playwrights' Center, 2001 PlayLabs), *Men & Boxes* and *Buying a House* (both winners in the Alliance of Los Angeles Playwrights new play competitions), *GreenHouse* (ASK Theater Projects), and *Tilting* (commissioned by The Will Geer Theatricum

Botanicum). *Unclaimed Assets* (from which "Fruit Flies" is taken) received its world premiere at the 2002 Edinburgh Fringe Festival.

Erin Cressida Wilson is a professor of English in the Creative Writing Program at Brown University and an internationally produced and award-winning playwright and screenwriter. She has written more than fifteen plays produced regionally, in New York City, and abroad at such stages as The Brooklyn Academy of Music, Joe's Pub at the Public Theatre, Classic Stage Company, Playwrights Horizons, Labyrinth Theatre, and the Traverse Theatre in Edinburgh. Her Off-Broadway productions include *The Trail of Her Inner Thigh, Hurricane, The Erotica Project* (coauthor), and the musical *Wilder* (cowritten with composers Jack Herrick and Mike Craver). In 2003, she won the Independent Spirit Award for her screenplay *Secretary*.

Betty Jane Wylie has published about twenty of her three dozen or so plays (that have been produced in theatres in Canada, the U.S., Britain, and New Zealand) in addition to more than thirty-five books, including biography, self-help, financial planning, inspiration, cookbooks, children's plays, puppet plays, belles letters, and poetry. She recently turned to film, and her first Movie of the Week won two Geminis (the Canadian equivalent of an Emmy).

Performance Rights

For Joan Ackerman, contact the author through Mary Narden, 870 Seventh Ave., Suite 905, New York, NY; 212-977-8421.

For Liz Duffy Adams, contact the author through Pat McLaughlin, Beacon Arts Agency, 208 West 30th Street #401, New York, NY 10001; 212-736-6630; beaconagency@hotmail.com.

For Janet Malia Allard, contact the author through The Playwright's Center, 2301 Franklin Ave. E., Minneapolis, MN 55406; 612-332-7481; www.pwcenter.org. Some scripts available through Playscripts, Inc., P.O. Box 237060, New York, NY 10023; 866-639-7529; www.playscripts.com.

For Rachel Axler, contact the author at rachel_axler@yahoo.com.

For Bianca Bagatourian, contact the author at biiianca@hotmail.com.

For Neena Beber, contact the author through New Dramatists, 424 W. 44th Street, New York, NY 10036; 212-757-6960; newdramatists@newdramatists.org.

For Brooke Berman, contact the author through New Dramatists, 424 W. 44th Street, New York, NY 10036; 212-757-6960; newdramatists@newdramatists.org.

For Meredith Besser, contact Heinemann, 361 Hanover Street, Portsmouth, NH 03801.

For Deborah Brevoort, contact the author at dbrevoort@aol.com or see the author's website at www.deborahbrevoort.com.

For Sharon Bridgforth, contact the author at sharon@sharonbridgforth.com.

For Kim Brundidge, contact the author at 1womnsho@bellsouth.net.

For Sheila Callaghan, contact the author at sheila_callaghan@hotmail.com.

For Darrah Cloud, contact the author through the Peregrine Whittlesey Agency, 345 E. 80th Street #31F, New York, NY 10021; 212-787-1802; pwwagy@aol.com.

For Constance Congdon, contact Heinemann, 361 Hanover Street, Portsmouth, NH 03801.

For Tönya Derrickson, contact the author at tmderrickson@yahoo.com.

For Constance Dial, contact the author at jmdcmd@aol.com.

For Donna Dinovelli, contact the author at ddinovelli@msn.com.

For Linda Eisenstein, contact the author through Herone Press, 1378 W. 64th Street, Cleveland, OH 44102; 216-961-5624; plays@lindaeisenstein.com.

For Annie Evans, contact the author through Mary Harden, Harden/Curtis Agency, 850 Seventh Ave., New York, NY 10019; 212-977-8502.

For Nell Grantham, contact the author through Ristau Entertainment, P.O. Box 7664, Roanoke, VA 24019; 540-556-5396; RistEntLtd@aol.com.

For Rinne Groff, contact the author through Val Day, William Morris Agency, 1325 Avenue of the Americas, New York, NY 10019; 212-903-1550; pfasst@wma.com.

For Ellen Hagan, contact Heinemann, 361 Hanover Street, Portsmouth, NH 03801.

For Imani M. Harrington, contact the author at Imandove202@hot mail.com.

For Jean Hedgecock, contact the author at jean@jeanhedgecock.com.

For Elizabeth Heffron, contact the author through the Peregrine Whittlesey Agency, 345 E. 80th Street #31F, New York, NY 10021; 212-737-0153; pwwagy@aol.com.

For Lindsay Brandon Hunter, contact the author at lindsaybrandon@hotmail.com.

For Carleen Jaspers contact the author at carleen.jaspers@k12.sd.us or crjaspers@yahoo.com.

For Susan Johnston, contact the author through Maura Teitelbaum, Abrams Artists Agency, 275 Seventh Ave., 26th floor, New York, NY 10001; 646-486-4600; maura.teitelbaum@abramsart.com. For scripts, contact Eldridge Plays & Musicals, P.O. Box 14367, Tallahassee, FL 32317; 800-HI-STAGE; info@histage.com.

For Honour Kane, contact the author through James Flynn, Jim Flynn Agency, 208 W. 30th Street, Suite 401, New York, NY 10001; 212-868-1068; Jimbbf@earthlink.net.

For Aurorae Khoo, contact the author through Josh Schechter, The Irv Schechter Agency, 9460 Wilshire Boulevard, Suite 300, Beverly Hills, CA 90212; 310-278-8070.

For Martha Kingsbury, contact Heinemann, 361 Hanover Street, Portsmouth, NH 03801.

For Lisa M. Konoplisky, contact the author at lmkbubba33@yahoo.com.

For Sherry Kramer, contact the author at SherryLKramer@aol.com.

For Mary R. Lathrop, contact the author at lathrop@sprynet.com.

For Michele Lowe, contact the author through Carl Mulert, The Joyce Ketay Agency, 630 Ninth Ave., Suite 706, New York, NY 10036; 212-354-6825. For scripts, contact Dramatic Publishing, P.O. Box 129, Woodstock, IL 60098-0129; 800-334-5302; www.dramaticpublishing.com.

For Ellen McLaughlin, contact the author through Joyce Ketay, The Joyce Ketay Agency, 630 Ninth Ave., Suite 706, New York, NY 10036; 212-354-6825; joyce@joyceketay.com.

For Ana Maria Mebane, contact the author at dscochintz@aol.com.

For Susan Mendelsohn, contact the author at sawmendelsohn@snet.net.

For S. P. Miskowski, contact the author at spmiskow@yahoo.com.

For Stephanie V. Moore, contact the author at steffiev@aol.com.

For Julie Marie Myatt, contact the author through Bruce Ostler, Bret Adams, Ltd., 448 W. 44th Street, New York, NY 10036; 212-765-5640; bostler.bal@verizon.net.

For Jamie Pachino Jones, contact the author through Writers & Artists, 19 W. 44th Street, Suite 1000, New York, NY; 212-391-1112.

For Regina M. Porter contact Heinemann, 361 Hanover Street, Portsmouth, NH 03801.

For Susanna Ralli, contact the author at susralli@aol.com.

For Jacquelyn Reingold, contact the author through Scott Yoselow, Gersh Agency, 41 Madison Ave., 33rd Floor, New York, NY 10010; 212-634-8102; syoselow@gershny.com.

For Tania Richard, contact the author at taniajr@webtv.net.

For Kate Robin, contact the author through Joyce Ketay, The Joyce Ketay Agency, 630 Ninth Avenue, Suite 706, New York, NY 10036; 212-354-6825; joyce@joyceketay.com.

For Sarah Ruhl, contact the author through Bruce Ostler, Bret Adams, Ltd., 448 W. 44th Street, New York, NY 10036; 212-765-5640; bostler.bal@verizon.net.

For Buffy Sedlachek, contact Heinemann, 361 Hanover Street, Portsmouth, NH 03801.

For Betty Shamieh, contact the author at bettyplaywright@yahoo.com.

For Jane Shepard, contact the author at jmershep@aol.com.

For Lillian Ann Slugocki, contact the author through Andrew Blauner, 12 E. 86th Street, Suite 633, New York, NY 10028; 212-772-0573; Blauner@aol.com.

For Caridad Svich, contact the author through New Dramatists, 424 W. 44th Street, New York, NY 10036; 212-757-6960; newdramatists@newdramastists.org.

For Colin Denby Swanson, contact the author through Maura Teitelbaum, Abrams Artists Agency, 275 Seventh Ave., 26th Floor, New York, NY 10001; 646-486-4600.

For Fiona J. Torres, contact the author at fiona_j_torres@msn.com.

For Jennie Webb, contact the author at jenniewebb@earthlink.net.

For Erin Cressida Wilson, contact the author through George Lane, Creative Artists Agency, 767 Fifth Ave., New York, NY 10153; 212-388-3600.

For Betty Jane Wylie, contact the author at beejay@muskoka.com.